The Four Week Ketogenic Bliss: For Meat Lovers

David Maxwell

Table of Contents

Introduction

Many readers may be unfamiliar with the ketogenic diet. This introduction discusses some general ideas about ketogenic diets, as well as defining terms that may be helpful. In the most general terms, a ketogenic diet is any diet that makes the liver produce ketone bodies, shifting the body's metabolism away from glucose and towards fat utilization. More specifically, a ketogenic diet is one that limits carbohydrates below a certain level (generally 100 grams per day), inducing a series of adaptations to take place. Protein and fat intake are changeable, depending on the goal of the dieter. However, the decisive criteria of whether a diet is ketogenic or not is the presence (or absence) of carbohydrates.

Fuel metabolism and the ketogenic diet

Normally, the body uses a combination of carbohydrates, protein and fat for energy. When carbohydrates are removed from the diet, the body's small stores are quickly depleted. As a result, the body is compelled to find an alternative fuel to provide energy. One of these fuels is free fatty acids (FFA), which can be utilized by most tissues in the body. However, not all organs can use FFA. For instance, the brain and nervous system are unable to utilize FFA for fuel ; however, they can use ketone bodies.

Ketone bodies are a by-product of the partial breakdown of FFA in the liver. They are used as as a non-carbohydrate, fat-derived energy source for tissues such as the brain. When ketone bodies are formed at fast rates, they mount up in the bloodstream, leading to a metabolic state called ketosis. At the same time, there is a decline in glucose utilization and production. Along with this, there is a decline in the breakdown of protein to be used for energy, referred to as 'protein sparing'. Many individuals are attracted towards ketogenic diets in an attempt to lose bodyfat while reducing the loss of lean body mass.

Hormones and the ketogenic diet

Ketogenic diets cause the effects described above primarily by changing levels of two hormones: insulin and glucagon. Insulin is a storage hormone, in charge of moving nutrients out of the bloodstream and into target tissues. For example, insulin causes glucose to be stored in muscle as glycogen, and FFA to be stored in adipose tissue as triglycerides. Glucagon is a fuel-mobilizing hormone, causing the body to break down stored glycogen, especially in the liver, to provide glucose for the body.

When carbohydrates are removed from the diet, insulin levels fall and glucagon levels rise. This causes a rise in FFA release from fat cells, and higher FFA burning in the liver. The quick burning of FFA in the liver is what eventually leads to the production of ketone bodies and the metabolic state of ketosis. Other than insulin and glucagon, a number of other hormones are also affected, all of which help to shift fuel use away from carbohydrates and towards fat.

Exercise and the ketogenic diet

As with any fat-loss diet, exercise goes well with the ketogenic diet. However, a diet without carbohydrates is unable to support high-intensity exercise performance, although low-intensity exercise may be performed. For this reason, individuals who wish to use a ketogenic diet and perform high-intensity exercise must add carbohydrates to the diet without disrupting the effects of ketosis. Two modified ketogenic diets are:

- The targeted ketogenic diet (TKD) permits carbohydrates to be consumed immediately around exercise, to support performance without affecting ketosis.
- The cyclical ketogenic diet (CKD) alternates periods of ketogenic dieting with periods of high-carbohydrate consumption. The period of high-carbohydrate eating refills muscle glycogen to support exercise performance.

What to Eat

One of the best parts of the keto diet is the food. I mean, seriously, all the bacon you can eat!! I have written another book called "The Four Week Paleo Challenge", and the meals in this Keto book are, by fat, more delicious than the meals in my Paleo book. It almost seems impossible that one might be able to lose weight eating such delicious food, but it is most definitely possible. The keto diet is one of the "easiest" diets to stick to for weight loss. However, you will need to avoid most packaged foods, since they are carbohydrate-based to improve shelf life. Your focus when grocery shopping should be on whole foods. This will reduce the risk of encountering hidden carbohydrates used as stabilizers in foods that may look keto-friendly, but are not. Following is an broad list of food that is appropriate for the keto diet.

MEAT

- Beef, all cuts
- Chicken, all cuts
- Cured meats
- Duck
- Eggs, all varieties
- Goose
- Lamb
- Offal (organ meat)
- Pork, all cuts
- Quail
- Veal
- Venison

NUTS & SEEDS

- Almonds

- Brazil nuts
- Cashews
- Chia seeds
- Flaxseeds
- Hazelnuts
- Hemp seeds
- Macadamias
- Peanuts
- Pecans
- Pistachios
- Pumpkin seeds
- Safflower seeds
- Sesame seeds
- Sunflower seeds
- Walnuts

SEAFOOD

- Bass
- Caviar
- Clams
- Crab
- Flounder
- Halibut
- Herring
- Lobster
- Mackerel
- Mussels
- Octopus
- Oysters
- Salmon
- Sardines
- Scallops
- Shrimp

- Squid
- Sole
- Tilapia
- Trout
- Tuna, fresh and canned

LOW GLYCEMIC FRUITS & VEGETABLES

- Arugula
- Asparagus
- Avocado
- Blackberries
- Bok choy
- Broccoli
- Broccoli raab
- Cabbage
- Cauliflower
- Celery
- Chicory greens
- Cilantro
- Cranberries
- Cucumber
- Eggplant
- Endive
- Fennel
- Garlic
- Green beans
- Jalapeño pepper
- Lemon
- Lettuce
- Lime
- Olives, green
- Parsley
- Radish

- Raspberries
- Rhubarb
- Spinach
- Sprouts, alfalfa and other small seeds
- Soybean
- Swiss
- chard
- Tomato
- Zucchini

MODERATE GLYCEMIC FRUITS & VEGETABLES

- Apple
- Artichoke
- Bell pepper
- Brussels sprouts
- Carrots, raw
- Celeriac
- Kale
- Kohlrabi
- Mushrooms
- Okra
- Onion
- Pumpkin
- Snow peas
- Spaghetti squash
- Strawberries
- Turnip
- Watermelon

FATS & OILS

- Almond butter
- Almond oil

- Avocado oil
- Butter
- Canola oil, in moderation
- Cocoa butter
- Coconut oil or MCT
- Fish oil, cod liver
- Flaxseed oil
- Grape seed oil
- Hemp seed oil
- Lard
- Macadamia oil
- Olive oil
- Peanut butter, sugar-free
- Peanut oil
- Safflower oil
- Sesame oil
- Soybean oil
- Sunflower butter
- Sunflower oil
- Vegetable oil, in moderation
- Walnut oil

DAIRY

- Almond milk, unsweetened
- Cheese, whole-milk varieties
- Coconut cream
- Coconut milk, unsweetened
- Cream cheese
- Greek yogurt, whole milk
- Heavy cream
- Sour cream
- Soy milk, unsweetened
- Whipped cream, unsweetened

What not to eat

Reducing carbohydrate intake is the foundation of inducing ketosis. Avoid any high-carbohydrate foods completely for best results with the keto diet. When we eat foods high in carbs, our bodies react by releasing insulin into the bloodstream to manage the increase in blood sugar created as those carbohydrates digest into sugar (glucose). If the glucose is not used efficiently for exercise, insulin forces the body to store it as fuel for later, which, in turn, becomes fat.

Grains and Legumes

Sadly for the bread lovers out there, it does not matter if it's whole wheat, organic, and sprouted—it still gets converted into sugar once it enters your body. This grain and legume category includes pasta, baked goods, rice, beans, chips, crackers, pizza crust, and cereal. Keep away from all grains, grain-based foods, and legumes (except peanuts) while adapting to keto due to their high-carbohydrate content.

Dairy

While dairy is a staple food for the keto diet, some dairy foods are loaded with carbohydrates. All milks (except those listed in the what to eat foods section) should be avoided, along with low-fat yogurt and cheese products. When shopping for dairy, look for grass-fed, full-fat options, which offer the most flavor and nutrients.

Most Fruits and Certain Vegetables

Fruit may seem like a clear healthy option when changing to a new diet, but most fruits cause a spike in insulin, which will end the state of ketosis. Fibrous vegetables are at the foundation of keto, and most vegetables with a high-fiber content can still be enjoyed. Outside of that, many staple vegetables lack fiber and also have high net carbohydrates. Vegetables like potatoes, corn, beets, peas, and winter squashes should be avoided.

Sugar

This seems obvious, but anything made with sugar is not allowed. Since keto depends on a low-insulin response from our bodies after we've eaten, anything with sugar will increase insulin thereby significantly reducing the effectiveness and benefits of the diet.

Low-Fat Foods

Briefly mentioned previously in the dairy section, low-fat foods are not favorable to the keto diet since they lack the very basis of it: fat.

The Four Week Diet Plan

Now that you have a general idea about the Ketogenic diet, we can dive right into the four week meal plan. I have written this book keeping in mind only meat lovers. There are a few veg recipes here and there, but the core of this diet plan is meat. You will not find this book one bit useful if you are vegetarian. However, if you love meat, and want to try the keto diet to lose fat, this is the book for you.

Nutritional info is provided at the end of every recipe. The value in the "Carbs" row does not contain fiber content. Considering how fiber is also a carbohydrate, it can be a little confusing so I am clarifying this beforehand. We only want to avoid the "Digestible" carbohydrates. Fiber goes well with the ketogenic diet as the body does not use it up for energy. Also, all nutritional info is Per Serving, unless stated otherwise.

All you need is Four weeks to get into a normal routine and then you'll be able to create great eating habits. Remember NOT to take 2 steps back every time you take one step forward. Stick to this meal plan for 4 weeks to see the results. It's easy to stick to it, much easier than sticking to my "Four Week Paleo Challenge" anyway.

Good luck on this journey and I hope that this meal plan helps you attain your goals.. The most delicious four weeks of your life begin now….

Week 1 Diet Plan

	Breakfast	Lunch	Dinner
M O N	Vanilla Butter Pound Cake (Pg 13)	WHITE CHILI (Pg 26)	BEEF AND BROCCOLI STIR-FRY (Pg 40)
T U E	BAKED EGGS IN HAM CUPS (Pg 1)	BANGERS AND CAULIFLOWER MASH (Pg 28)	BAKED "SPAGHETTI" (Pg 42)
W E D	BACON, EGG, AND CHEESE CUPS (Pg 16)	CHICKEN CORDON BLEU (Pg 30)	HERB-CRUSTED LAMB CHOPS (Pg 44)
T H U	Walnut Muffins (Pg 18)	ZUCCHINI MEATLOAF (Pg 32)	ROASTED TROUT WITH SWISS CHARD (Pg 46)
F R I	CRUSTLESS QUICHE LORRAINE (Pg 20)	CHICKEN PARMESAN (Pg34)	CLASSIC MOZZARELLA STICKS (Pg 48)
S A T	Nutty Breakfast Bars (Pg 22)	BAKED CHEESY MEATBALLS (Pg 36)	ROASTED COD WITH GARLIC BUTTER AND BOK CHOY (Pg 50)
S U N	BROCCOLI AND CHEESE QUICHE CUPS (Pg 24)	TOFU FRIES (Pg 38)	SMOKED SALMON AVOCADO SUSHI ROLL (Pg 52)

Week 1 Cookbook

Vanilla Butter Pound Cake

Yield: 12 Slices

Requirements:

- ½ lb. Unsalted Butter
- 1 ½ cup Almond Flour
- 3 Large Eggs
- 3 Egg Yolks
- ⅓ cup Erythritol
- ½ Tbsp. Vanilla Extract
- ½ tsp. Salt

Directions:

1. Bring all ingredients to room temperature, and once they are, preheat oven to 325F.
2. Little by little, mix the egg yolks, eggs, and vanilla. You only want to break the egg yolks, you don't want to let any air slip in.
3. Beat the soft butter on high, slowly adding the Erythritol. This should take around 4-5 minutes, changing the butter nearly white in color.
4. Turn on your mixer and run it on the lowest speed. Slowly add the egg mixture and salt to the butter.
5. Sift half the almond flour into the batter and fold it in. Repeat with the second half.
6. Cut some baking or parchment paper to coat the inside of a 9x4 bread pan.

7.   Butter the bread pan and add the baking or parchment paper.

8.   Bake for 60 minutes until it is golden brown and tester comes out clean. After 10 minutes, take out the cake from loaf pan.

9.   Wrap in plastic wrap and store at room temperature for at least 24 hours.

Nutritional Info	
Fats	24g
Carbs	1.4g
Protein	4.6g

BAKED EGGS IN HAM CUPS

Yield: 2 Servings

Requirements:

- Cooking spray for cupcake pan
- 4 slices Black Forest ham
- 4 eggs
- 1 teaspoon dried parsley

Directions:

1. Preheat your oven to 400°F.
2. Spray the cupcake pan with cooking spray.
3. Insert one slice of ham into each cup. The ham should hang over the sides.
4. Crack and pour one egg into each cup and garnish each with the parsley.
5. Put the cupcake pan in the preheated oven and cook for about 15 minutes, until the egg whites are cooked but the yolk is still slightly fluid.

Nutritional Info(total for 2 servings)	
Fats	28g
Carbs	6g
Fiber	0.8g
Protein	20.5g

BACON, EGG, AND CHEESE CUPS

Yield: 4 Servings

Requirements:

- 6 bacon slices, divided
- 4 eggs, beaten
- ½ cup heavy (whipping) cream
- ¼ teaspoon salt
- ⅛ teaspoon freshly ground black pepper
- ½ cup shredded Monterey Jack cheese, divided

Directions:

1.   Preheat your oven to 350°F.
2.   Take 4 cupcake tins and coat the side walls on the inside of the tins with one bacon slice each. Leave the bottom of the cup bare, for now.
3.   Slice the remaining two bacon slices into 2-inch pieces. Place 2 to 3 bacon pieces at the bottom of each bacon-wrapped cupcake tin so each is completely covered.
4.   In a medium bowl, mix together the eggs, heavy cream, salt, and pepper.
5.   Pour the egg mixture uniformly into the bacon-wrapped tins. Top each with 2 tablespoons of cheese.
6.   Cautiously place the cupcake pan in the oven to avoid spilling.
7.   Bake for 35 minutes or until golden brown.

Nutritional Info (Per Egg Cup)	
Fats	29g
Carbs	1.5g
Fiber	0g
Protein	22.5g

Walnut Muffins

Yield: 6 Muffins

Requirements:

- 1 cup Blanched Almond Flour
- 2 Large eggs
- 2 Tbsp. Erythritol
- 5 Drops Stevia
- ½ tsp. Baking Soda
- 1 tsp. Apple Cider Vinegar
- 1 cup Walnuts
- 4 Lindt 98% Cacao Squares

Directions:

1. Preheat your oven to 350F.
2. Slice the chocolate into small chunks.
3. Mix almond flour, baking soda and erythritol in one bowl.
4. Combine the eggs, Stevia, and vinegar in another bowl.
5. Gradually add the dry ingredients to the wet while stirring together.
6. Once mixed, fold the chocolate and walnuts into the mixture.
7. Pour the mixture evenly into 6 cupcake liners inside a cupcake pan using a spoon.
8. Bake for 15 minutes, or until they are golden brown on the top.
9. Let them cool for 15-20 minutes.

Nutritional Info(total for 6 muffins)	
Fats	20.5g
Carbs	3.1g
Protein	7.7g

CRUSTLESS QUICHE LORRAINE

Yield: 8 Servings

Requirements:

- Cooking spray for pie pan
- 1 pound thick-cut bacon, grease reserved
- 1 tablespoon minced garlic
- ¼ cup minced onion
- 4 eggs, beaten
- 1½ cups heavy (whipping) cream
- 1 cup shredded Swiss cheese
- ½ cup shredded Gruyère cheese
- ¾ teaspoon salt
- ¼ teaspoon freshly ground black pepper

Directions:

1. Preheat your oven to 350°F.
2. Lightly spray the pie pan. In a large skillet over medium-high heat, cook the bacon for 6 to 8 minutes, until crunchy.
3. Take the bacon out of the skillet to drain on paper towels, preserving the remaining bacon grease in the skillet. Once cooled, slice the bacon into small pieces and set aside.
4. To the left over grease in the skillet with the heat lowered to medium, add the minced garlic and onions.
5. Cook for 3 to 4 minutes, browning slightly, and then turn off heat.
6. Pour the onion and garlic mixture into a small bowl. Set aside to cool.
7. In a large bowl, beat the eggs and heavy cream with a whisk for 2 minutes to mix completely.
8. Add the Swiss and Gruyère cheeses, reserved bacon, onions and garlic, salt, and pepper to the egg mixture and mix well.

9. Gradually pour the egg mixture into the prepared pie pan.

10. Cautiously place the pan on the middle rack in the oven. Bake for 20 to 25 minutes, until the center has solidified.

11. Take the pan out of the oven.

12. Cool the quiche for 5 minutes before slicing and serving.

Nutritional Info PER SERVING (⅛ OF QUICHE)	
Fats	42.7g
Carbs	2.3g
Fiber	0g
Protein	22.1g

Nutty Breakfast Bars

Yield: 4 Bars

Requirements:

- ½ cup Walnuts
- ½ cup Pistachios
- 1/4 cup Coconut Oil
- 1/4 cup Peanut Butter
- 1/4 cup Flax Seed Meal
- 1/4 tsp. Almond Extract
- 7 Drops Liquid Stevia

Directions:

1. Crush the nuts and toast them in a pan over medium-low heat. While the nuts are toasting, place the coconut oil and peanut butter into a microwave safe container.
2. Microwave the oil and peanut butter for 25 seconds until it is completely melted.
3. Combine the oil and peanut butter with the Stevia and almond extract.
4. Once the nuts are toasted, arrange them in a 9x4 dish.
5. Sprinkle 1/4 Cup Flax over the nuts, and then pour the peanut butter and oil mixture over the nuts.
6. Place the mixture into the freezer for a minimum of 4 hours, until it turns solid and then chop it into 4 bars.

Nutritional Info Per Serving

Fats	40.5g
Carbs	4g
Protein	10.5g

BROCCOLI AND CHEESE QUICHE CUPS

Yield: 4 QUICHE CUPS

Requirements:

- Cooking spray for ramekins
- ½ teaspoon salt, plus additional for salting the cooking water
- 1½ cups broccoli florets
- 5 eggs
- ¾ cup heavy (whipping) cream
- ¼ teaspoon freshly ground black pepper
- ½ teaspoon minced garlic
- ¾ cup shredded sharp Cheddar cheese

Directions:

1. Preheat your oven to 350°F.
2. Spray four ramekins with cooking spray and lay them on a baking sheet.
3. Boil a medium pot of salted water and add the broccoli and cook for 1 minute. Drain the broccoli from the pot and use paper towels to completely drain it.
4. Slice the drained broccoli and set aside.
5. In a large bowl, mix together the eggs, heavy cream, salt, and pepper.
6. Fold in the broccoli, garlic, and cheese.
7. Split the egg mixture evenly among the prepared ramekins. Lay the baking sheet with the ramekins into the preheated oven.
8. Bake until the egg and broccoli mixture has risen and is slightly browned, about 35 minutes.

Nutritional Info (1 quiche cup)	
Fats	21.1g
Carbs	3.8g
Fiber	0.9g
Protein	13.7g

WHITE CHILI

Yield: 12 Servings

Requirements:

- ½ cup butter
- 2 cups chopped onion
- 2 cups peeled, cubed turnips
- 1½ cups diced red bell pepper
- ½ cup diced orange or yellow bell pepper
- 1 (3-ounce) can diced green chiles
- 4 garlic cloves, minced
- 2 pounds ground chicken
- 5 cups chicken broth
- 2 teaspoons chili powder (or to taste)
- 2 teaspoons cumin
- 2 teaspoons oregano
- 1 teaspoon cayenne pepper
- 1 teaspoon salt
- 1 teaspoon freshly ground black pepper
- 16 ounces sour cream
- 2 cups shredded Cheddar cheese

Directions:

1. Melt the butter in a large stockpot over medium-high heat and add the onion. Gently heat for 8 to 10 minutes, stirring occasionally.
2. Put in the turnips, red bell pepper, orange bell pepper, green chiles, and garlic. Sauté for 5 to 6 minutes.
3. Put in the ground chicken and stir to break up the meat, browning on all sides for 6 to 8 minutes.
4. Pour in the chicken broth and stir to combine.

5.　Put in the chili powder, cumin, oregano, and cayenne pepper. Bring to a boil. Turn the heat to low.

6.　Cook the chili for 6 to 8 hours, until reduced and thickened. Add salt and black pepper to taste.

7.　Serve with the sour cream and Cheddar cheese.

Nutritional Info Per Serving	
Fats	28.3g
Carbs	8.4g
Fiber	1.6g
Protein	30.6g

BANGERS AND CAULIFLOWER MASH

Yield: 4 Servings

Requirements:

- 8 Italian sausage links
- ½ teaspoon salt
- ¼ teaspoon freshly ground black pepper
- 2 tablespoons olive oil
- 2 tablespoons butter
- 1½ cups sliced onions
- 1 cup beef stock
- 2 tablespoons sherry (optional)
- ¼ cup heavy (whipping) cream
- Cauliflower Mash for serving

Directions:

1. Brown the sausages on all sides in a large skillet over high heat. Should take around 5 to 7 minutes. While cooking, add salt and pepper to taste. Once done, transfer to a plate and set aside.
2. In the same large skillet, over medium-high heat, heat the olive oil and butter for around 1 minute. Put in the onions and cook until they brown. Should take about 7 minutes.
3. Put in the beef stock and sherry (if using) to the skillet with inions. Stir to combine and bring to a boil and cook to reduce the liquid. Should take about 4 minutes.
4. Reduce the heat to medium and add the heavy cream to the onion mixture and cook for another 2 to 3 minutes.
5. Return the sausages and any accumulated juices to the skillet and cook for 1 minute.
6. Plate two sausages with a serving of Cauliflower Mash per person.

Nutritional Info	
Fats	52.3g
Carbs	105g
Fiber	2.9g
Protein	17.8g

CHICKEN CORDON BLEU

Yield: 8 Servings

Requirements:

- Cooking spray for the baking dish
- 18 ounces thinly sliced chicken thighs (about 8 pieces)
- 8 ounces pork rinds
- ¼ cup grated Parmesan cheese
- ½ teaspoon dried parsley
- ½ teaspoon dried oregano
- ½ teaspoon dried basil
- ¼ teaspoon dried rosemary
- ¼ teaspoon garlic powder
- ¼ teaspoon onion powder
- ¼ teaspoon crushed red pepper flakes
- ¼ teaspoon salt
- ¼ teaspoon freshly ground black pepper
- 2 eggs
- 3 ounces (3 slices) deli ham, halved, divided
- 2 ounces (3 slices) Swiss cheese, halved, divided
- 8 tablespoons (1 stick) butter, divided

Directions:

1. Preheat your oven to 450°F.
2. Coat the baking dish with cooking spray.
3. On a level surface, put the chicken thighs between two pieces of plastic wrap. Pound the chicken until the pieces are all about ¼ inch thick. Set aside.
4. In a food processor, beat the pork rinds into a fine powder and transfer to a large bowl.

5. Add the Parmesan cheese, parsley, oregano, basil, rosemary, garlic powder, onion powder, red pepper flakes, salt, and pepper to the ground pork rinds and mix the coating thoroughly.

6. In a medium bowl, beat the eggs.

7. Line up the egg wash, then the pork rind mixture, then the prepared baking dish.

8. On a level surface, lay out each chicken breast. On the top of each breast, place one-half slice of ham and one-half slice of Swiss cheese. Top each with 1 tablespoon of butter. Roll up each breast, finishing seam-side down.

9. Cautiously immerse one chicken roll into the egg wash, then coat completely with the pork rind mixture, pressing firmly. Put the breaded chicken roll seam-side down into the prepared pan. Repeat the process with the remaining chicken rolls.

10. Lay the pan in the oven. Bake for 25 to 30 minutes, until golden brown.

Nutritional Info (1 CHICKEN ROLL)	
Fats	32.6g
Carbs	1.6g
Fiber	0.3g
Protein	45.3g

ZUCCHINI MEATLOAF

Yield: 7 Servings

Requirements:

- 1 pound 80-percent lean ground beef
- ½ pound bacon, chopped
- 1 zucchini, finely chopped
- 1 onion, finely chopped
- 3 tablespoons tomato paste
- 2 eggs
- 1 tablespoon Dijon mustard
- ¼ teaspoon paprika
- ¼ teaspoon salt
- ¼ teaspoon freshly ground black pepper
- 1¼ cups almond flour
- Cooking spray for loaf pan

Directions:

1. Preheat your oven to 350°F.
2. In a large bowl, mix the ground beef, bacon, zucchini, and onion.
3. Put in the tomato paste, eggs, mustard, paprika, salt, and pepper and mix well.
4. Add the almond flour and mix again, making sure there are no clusters.
5. Pour the beef mixture to a loaf pan coated with cooking spray. Cover with aluminum foil and put in the preheated oven and cook for 1 hour.
6. Take the loaf out of the oven, remove the foil, and put the loaf back into the oven.
7. Increase the heat to broil and cook for 10 minutes, or until the top is browned.

8. Take the pan out of the oven and let the meatloaf to cool in the pan for 5 minutes.
9. Remove the meatloaf using a knife.
10. Slice into 7 equal slices and serve.

Nutritional Info	
Fats	36.9g
Carbs	4.8g
Fiber	3.2g
Protein	32g

CHICKEN PARMESAN

Yield: Servings 6

Requirements:

- 3 large boneless chicken breasts, halved
- ¾ cup grated Parmesan cheese, divided
- ½ cup almond flour
- 1 teaspoon Italian seasoning
- ½ teaspoon garlic powder
- ¼ teaspoon salt
- ⅛ teaspoon freshly ground black pepper
- 1 egg
- ¼ cup olive oil
- 6 tablespoons sugar-free Pasta Sauce , divided
- 1 cup shredded mozzarella cheese, divided

Directions:

1. Preheat your oven to 350°F.
2. Put the chicken between two pieces of plastic wrap. Pound the chicken and flatten until all pieces are about ½ inch thick.
3. In a medium bowl, combine ½ cup of Parmesan cheese, the almond flour, Italian seasoning, garlic powder, salt, and pepper.
4. In an additional bowl, beat the egg.
5. Line up the egg wash, then the Parmesan coating. Immerse each piece of chicken into the egg wash and set aside.
6. In a large skillet over medium-high heat, heat the olive oil for about 2 minutes. Add the coated chicken and cook for 5 to 7 minutes, or until browned on each side.
7. Take the chicken out of the skillet and place on a parchment-lined baking sheet.

8. Top with 1 tablespoon of Pasta Sauce and divide the 1 cup of mozzarella cheese among the chicken. Sprinkle each with the remaining Parmesan cheese.

9. Put the baking sheet in the oven. Bake for 20 minutes, until the cheese is thoroughly melted.

Nutritional Info PER SERVING (½ CHICKEN BREAST WITH SAUCE AND CHEESE)	
Fats	30g
Carbs	4g
Fiber	1.3g
Protein	44g

BAKED CHEESY MEATBALLS

Yield: 3 Servings

Requirements:

- ½ pound 80-percent lean ground beef
- ½ pound ground pork
- ½ cup grated Parmesan cheese
- ¼ cup almond flour
- 2 tablespoons water
- 1 tablespoon minced garlic
- ½ teaspoon salt
- ¼ teaspoon freshly ground black pepper
- 1 tablespoon olivey oil
- 2 tablespoons butter
- 1½ cups Pasta Sauce , or purchased sugar-free marinara
- ¾ cup shredded mozzarella cheese
- Fresh parsley for garnish

Directions:

1.   Preheat your oven to 400°F.
2.   In a large bowl, thoroughly mix the ground beef, pork, Parmesan cheese, almond flour, water, garlic, salt, and pepper. Form the meat into about 10 small meatballs.
3.   Heat the olive oil and butter for about 1 minute In a large skillet over medium-high heat,.
4.   Put the meatballs into the skillet and brown on all sides, about 2 minutes per side. Take out of the skillet and set aside.
5.   In an oven-safe dish, lay the meatballs so that they just fill up the whole dish.

6. Coat the meatballs with the Pasta Sauce. Put the mozzarella on top of the meatballs evenly.

7. Put the dish into the preheated oven. Bake for 15 to 20 minutes, until the cheese browns and the internal temperature of the meatballs is 170°F.

8. Garnish with the parsley, and serve.

Nutritional Info	
Fats	39.8g
Carbs	9.7g
Fiber	2.1g
Protein	62.1g

TOFU FRIES

Yield: 2 Servings

Requirements:

- Oil for frying
- 1 package (12 ounces) extra-firm tofu, sliced into ¼-inch slices
- 1 tablespoon salt
- 2 teaspoons freshly ground black pepper
- 1 teaspoon ground cumin
- 1 teaspoon dried parsley
- 1 teaspoon garlic powder
- ½ teaspoon onion powder
- ¼ teaspoon paprika
- ¼ teaspoon cayenne pepper
- Sugar-Free Ketchup for serving

Directions:

1. Take four inches of oil in a large pot and heat it to 350°F.
2. Thoroughly dry each tofu slice using paper towels or a dishcloth.
3. In a medium bowl, combine the salt, black pepper, cumin, parsley, garlic powder, onion powder, paprika, and cayenne pepper and mix well.
4. Dip the tofu fries in the spice mixture once and set aside.
5. Working in batches, put in a few fries at a time to the oil so they do not stick together and cook each batch for about 4 minutes, or until golden brown. Take out of the oil with a slotted spoon. Set aside and let it drain on paper towels.
6. Replicate the process with the remaining tofu strips, working in batches as needed.
7. Serve with Sugar-Free Ketchup .

Nutritional Info	
Fats	14.3g
Carbs	4g
Fiber	2.5g
Protein	14.7g

BEEF AND BROCCOLI STIR-FRY

Yield: 4 Servings

Requirements:

- 2 tablespoons soy sauce
- 2 garlic cloves, minced
- 2 tablespoons sake
- 1 tablespoon grated fresh ginger
- ½ teaspoon Chinese five-spice powder
- 1 (1-pound) skirt steak, sliced into 1-inch strips, then halved crosswise
- 3 tablespoons coconut oil
- 1 cup diced onion
- 4 cups broccoli florets
- ½ cup sliced scallions

Directions:

1. In a large bowl, mix together the soy sauce, garlic, sake, ginger, and five-spice powder. Add the steak strips. Cover. Refrigerate to marinate for at least 15 minutes.
2. In a large deep skillet or wok over medium-high heat, heat the coconut oil for about 1 minute. Put in the onion and sauté for 2 minutes, or until tender.
3. Put the beef and marinade into the skillet and cook for 4 to 5 minutes, stirring occasionally.
4. Put the broccoli and scallions into the skillet and sauté for 2 minutes. Cover and reduce the heat to medium-low and cook, covered, for another 2 to 3 minutes, or until the broccoli is tender.
5. Mix the ingredients thoroughly, and serve.

Nutritional Info	
Fats	22g
Carbs	11.8g
Fiber	3.5g
Protein	34g

BAKED "SPAGHETTI"

Yield: 8 Servings

Requirements:

- 1 large spaghetti squash (yields 5 cups)
- ½ cup butter
- ½ pound 80-percent lean ground beef
- ½ pound Italian sausage
- ½ pound chicken sausage
- ½ cup red wine
- 1 large onion, diced
- 5 garlic cloves, minced
- ½ pound mushrooms, sliced
- 1 (6-ounce) can tomato paste
- 1 (18-ounce) can diced tomatoes
- 1 tablespoon Italian seasoning
- 4 ounces ricotta cheese, divided
- 4 ounces mozzarella cheese, divided
- 8 ounces grated Parmesan cheese, divided
- ½ teaspoon salt
- ½ teaspoon freshly ground black pepper

Directions:

1. Preheat your oven to 350°F.
2. Put the spaghetti squash in a large microwaveable bowl and use the tip of a sharp knife to pierce the shell all around. Microwave on high for 15 to 20 minutes, depending on the size of your squash. Take out of the microwave and set aside to cool.
3. Heat a large skillet over medium-high heat and add the butter. Melt for 1 to 2 minutes.

4.   Put the ground beef, Italian sausage, and chicken sausage into the pan and sauté for about 10 minutes.

5.   Put in the red wine and reduce the heat to medium, allowing the wine reduce with the meat for 3 to 5 minutes.

6.   Put in the onion and garlic and cook until tender, about 4 minutes. Add the mushrooms and stir, cooking for an additional 8 to 9 minutes.

7.   Put in the tomato paste, diced tomatoes with the juices, and Italian seasoning to the mixture and mix thoroughly and cook for 10 to 15 minutes, until reduced by half.

8.   Go back to the spaghetti squash. Cut it in half lengthwise. Clean it, removing the inner seeds, and scrape out the flesh with a fork.

9.   In a large baking dish with a lid, spread half of the spaghetti squash in the bottom. Put 2 ounces of ricotta, 2 ounces of mozzarella, and 4 ounces of Parmesan on top. Coat with the tomato sauce. Pour the remaining half of the spaghetti squash on top.

10. Finish with the remaining 2 ounces of ricotta, 2 ounces of mozzarella, and 4 ounces of Parmesan cheese.

11. Cover the pan and place it in the preheated oven. Bake for 20 minutes.

12. Take the dish out of the oven and carefully remove the lid. Return the uncovered dish to the oven and bake for another 15 to 20 minutes. Finish with 2 to 3 minutes under the broiler for a crispy, browned top. Allow it to cool for 10 to 15 minutes before serving.

Nutritional Info	
Fats	32.5g
Carbs	9.1g
Fiber	6.1g
Protein	33.7g

HERB-CRUSTED LAMB CHOPS

Yield: 3 Servings

Requirements:

- 1 pound lamb chops
- 2 tablespoons Dijon mustard
- 4 fresh rosemary sprigs, chopped
- 4 fresh thyme sprigs, chopped
- 3 tablespoons almond flour
- 4 garlic cloves, minced
- 1 teaspoon onion powder
- ¼ teaspoon salt
- ¼ teaspoon freshly ground black pepper
- 4 tablespoons olive oil, divided

Directions:

1. Preheat your oven to 350°F.
2. Cover the lamb chops with the mustard and set aside.
3. Add the rosemary, thyme, almond flour, garlic, onion powder, salt, and pepper to a blender or food processor and pulse until finely chopped.
4. Gradually add about 2 tablespoons of olive oil to form a thick paste.
5. Press the herb paste tightly around the edges of the mustard-coated chops, creating a crust.
6. Heat the remaining 2 tablespoons of olive oil for 2 minutes in a large oven-safe skillet over medium heat.
7. Put the chops into the skillet on their sides to brown.
8. Cook, undisturbed, for 2 to 3 minutes so the crust sticks properly to the meat.
9. Rotate and cook on the opposite edge for 2 to 3 minutes more.
10. Transfer the chops to a baking sheet.

11. Lay the sheet in the preheated oven and cook for 7 to 8 minutes, for medium.

12. Take the sheet out of the oven and serve immediately.

Nutritional Info(Per Serving)	
Fats	32.1g
Carbs	2.6g
Fiber	1.3g
Protein	43.3g

ROASTED TROUT WITH SWISS CHARD

Yield: 4 Servings

Requirements:

- 1 teaspoon salt, divided
- ½ teaspoon freshly ground black pepper, divided
- 4 (8-ounce) trout, cleaned
- 4 fresh dill sprigs
- 4 fresh fennel sprigs
- 2 pounds Swiss chard, cleaned and leaves separated from stems
- 4 tablespoons olive oil, divided
- 4 tablespoons butter, divided
- 1 lemon, quartered
- 4 tablespoons dry vermouth, or white wine, divided

Directions:

1.   Preheat your oven to 450°F.
2.   Season the insides of the trout with ½ teaspoon of salt and ¼ teaspoon of pepper. Put 1 dill sprig and 1 fennel sprig inside each trout.
3.   Divide the Swiss chard stems into 2-inch pieces. Chop the leaves crosswise into 1½-inch strips. Set aside.
4.   Cut four large pieces of aluminum foil into oval shapes large enough to fit one trout and one-quarter of the Swiss chard, with room enough to be sealed.
5.   Using ¾ tablespoon of olive oil, brush the trout. Put one trout in the center of each piece of foil.
6.   Put each trout on top with one-quarter of the Swiss chard.

7.   Season the trout with the remaining ½ teaspoon of salt, ¼ teaspoon of pepper, and 3¼ tablespoons of olive oil. Put 1 tablespoon of butter on top of each tout.

8.   Squeeze a lemon quarter over every Swiss chard and trout bundle. Spoon 1 tablespoon of vermouth above each, as well. Close and seal the foil pouches tightly.

9.   Lay the foil packets on a baking sheet. Bake in the preheated oven for 10 to 12 minutes, depending on the thickness of the fish.

10. Remove from the oven and allow the packets to cool for 1 to 2 minutes before opening. Serve in the foil packet.

Nutritional Info PER SERVING (1 TROUT, ¼ SWISS CHARD)	
Fats	36.1g
Carbs	7g
Fiber	4.4g
Protein	43.6g

CLASSIC MOZZARELLA STICKS

Yield: 4 Servings

Requirements:

- 2 ounces powdered Parmesan cheese
- 1 teaspoon Italian seasoning
- 1 egg
- 5 mozzarella cheese sticks
- Oil for frying
- Pizza Sauce or Ranch Dressing for serving

Directions:

1.   In a large bowl, mix the powdered Parmesan cheese and Italian seasoning.
2.   In another bowl, whisk the egg for 1 minute.
3.   On a cutting board, chop each mozzarella stick crosswise into 3 parts for 15 pieces total.
4.   Plunge one piece of the mozzarella into the egg and then roll it in the seasoned Parmesan cheese.
5.   Again dip the piece of cheese in the egg, and then again in the Parmesan cheese.
6.   Roll the cheese-covered mozzarella piece between your hands so the coating sticks.
7.   Repeat with remaining mozzarella pieces.
8.   Freeze the cheese sticks for at least 1 hour.
9.   When ready to cook, preheat 1 inch of oil in a large pan to 350°F.
10.   Put 2 to 3 cheese sticks in the pan at a time and cook for 2 to 3 minutes, turn, and cook for 2-3 minutes again.
11.   Transfer to paper towels to drain.

12. Replicate the process with the remaining pieces.
13. Serve with Pizza Sauce or Ranch Dressing .

Nutritional Info PER SERVING (ABOUT 4 PIECES)	
Fats	22g
Carbs	2g
Fiber	0g
Protein	21g

ROASTED COD WITH GARLIC BUTTER AND BOK CHOY

Yield: 2 Servings

Requirements:

- 2 (8-ounce) cod fillets
- ¼ cup (½ stick) butter, thinly sliced
- 1 tablespoon minced garlic
- ½ pound baby bok choy, halved lengthwise
- ¼ teaspoon salt
- ¼ teaspoon freshly ground black pepper

Directions:

1. Preheat your oven to 400°F.
2. Make a large pouch from aluminum foil and place the cod fillets inside and evenly put slices of butter and the garlic on top.
3. Tuck the bok choy around the fillets and add salt and pepper to taste.
4. Close the pouch with the two ends of the foil joining at the top, so the butter stays in the pouch.
5. Put the sealed pouches in a baking dish. Place the dish in the preheated oven, and bake for 15 to 20 minutes, depending on the thickness of the fillets.
6. Take the dish out of the oven and check the fillets for doneness.
7. Serve immediately.

Nutritional Info (1 COD FILLET, ½ OF THE BOK CHOY)	
Fats	24g
Carbs	2.7g
Fiber	1.3g
Protein	23g

SMOKED SALMON AVOCADO SUSHI ROLL

Yield: 4 Servings

Requirements:

- 14 ounces smoked salmon
- 1 tablespoon wasabi paste (optional)
- ¾ cup cream cheese, at room temperature
- ½ avocado, sliced
- 1 tablespoon sesame seeds

Directions:

1. Lay out a large piece of plastic wrap on a cutting board.
2. Put the salmon pieces on the plastic wrap, overlapping, to create a large rectangle 6 to 7 inches long and 4 inches wide.
3. In a small bowl, combine the wasabi paste (if using) and the cream cheese.
4. Spread the cream cheese evenly over the entire smoked salmon rectangle.
5. Position the avocado over the cream cheese, in the center of the rectangle.
6. Holding the plastic wrap at one end, lift and cautiously begin to roll the salmon. Hold the plastic wrap firmly over the roll as you go to apply pressure to hold it together.
7. Unwrap the plastic wrap from the sushi roll.
8. Coat the sushi roll with sesame seeds, patting them into the outer layer.
9. Refrigerate the roll for 15 to 20 minutes.
10. With a very sharp knife, chop into pieces and serve.

Nutritional Info	
Fats	24g
Carbs	6.6g
Fiber	5.7g
Protein	31.3g

Week 2 Diet Plan

	BREAKFAST	LUNCH	DINNER
M O N	**RADISH SCRAMBLE (Pg 55)**	**CILANTRO CHILI CHICKEN SKEWERS** (Pg 69)	**FIVE-ALARM BEEF CHILI** (Pg 83)
T U E	**CHEESY AVOCADO BAKED EGGS (Pg 57)**	**BEEF FAJITAS** (Pg 71)	**BARBECUE ONION AND GOAT CHEESE FLATBREAD** (Pg 85)
W E D	**BACON KETO PANCAKES (Pg 59)**	**AVOCADO CHICKEN BURGER** (Pg 73)	**SESAME BROILED CHICKEN THIGHS** (Pg 87)
T H U	**BACON-WRAPPED ASPARAGUS AND EGGS (Pg 61)**	**POT ROAST WITH TURNIPS AND RADISHES** (Pg 75)	**GROUND BEEF TACO SALAD** (Pg 89)
F R I	**STEAK AND EGGS (Pg 63)**	**CURRIED CHICKEN** (Pg 77)	**BACON RANCH CHEESY CHICKEN BREASTS** (Pg 91)
S A T	**SCOTCH EGGS (Pg 65)**	**BEEF STROGANOFF** (Pg 79)	**PHILLY CHEESESTEAK STUFFED PEPPERS** (Pg 93)
S U N	**SPAGHETTI SQUASH PANCAKES (Pg 67)**	**JAMAICAN JERK CHICKEN** (Pg 81)	**CHICKEN FAJITA STUFFED BELL PEPPERS** (Pg 95)

Week 2 Cookbook

Radish Scramble

Yield: 2 Servings

Requirements:

- 8 Oz Flank Steak
- 6 Oz. Radishes
- 2 Oz Cubetti Pancetta
- 4 Oz Cheddar Cheese
- 4 Eggs
- Salt and Pepper to taste

Directions:

1.   Preheat your oven to 450 degrees.
2.   Pan fry the flank steak for 90 seconds, flip, and fry for another 90 seconds. Set aside.
3.   Rinse the radishes, then chop off the ends and quarter.
4.   Brown the radishes and pancetta in a skillet or pan that can fit into your oven. Browning should take about 6 minutes.
5.   Chop the flank steak and add into the pan.
6.   Put the cheese and break the eggs into the mixture, season to taste and cook for a minute to set the bottom of the pan.
7.   Put the pan insude the oven and cook for 8 minutes, broiling for an additional 4 minutes or until the eggs are set to the desired level.

Nutritional Info	
Fats	55g
Carbs	5g
Fiber	1g
Protein	64g

CHEESY AVOCADO BAKED EGGS

Yield: 2 Servings

Requirements:

- 1 avocado, halved lengthwise, pitted
- 2 eggs
- 4 tablespoons shredded Colby cheese, divided
- ⅛ teaspoon salt, divided
- ⅛ teaspoon freshly ground black pepper, divided

Directions:

1. Preheat your oven to 475°F.
2. Scrape out enough avocado from each half so an egg fits. Place all avocado halves in a ramekin, setting it into the ramekin, cut side facing up. Using two small bowls, cautiously crack an egg into each. Do not break the yolk.
3. Spoon one yolk into each avocado half and fill to the top with egg white.
4. Sprinkle 2 tablespoons of Colby cheese on each avocado half. Add salt and pepper to taste.
5. Place the ramekins in the preheated oven vigilantly so the avocado halves don't turn over.
6. Bake 15 to 20 minutes, or to your desired doneness.

Nutritional Info	
PER SERVING (1 AVOCADO HALF WITH EGG AND CHEESE FILLING)	
Fats	28.5g
Carbs	2.7g
Fiber	6.8g
Protein	11g

Bacon Keto Pancakes

Yield: 8 Pancakes, Serving size: 2 pancakes

Requirements:

- 1 Cup Carbquik
- 1 Egg
- ½ Cup Heavy Cream
- ¼ Cup Water
- ½ Cup Unsalted Butter, Melted
- 1 Tbsp Sugar Free Vanilla Syrup
- ½ Tsp Baking Soda
- 8 Slices Bacon

Directions:

- Cook bacon as you prefer- in the oven or on the stove.
- Melt butter in a microwave.
- Combine the Carbquik and the baking soda.
- Add all other liquid ingredients and stir well until mixed.
- Heat pan over medium-high heat and then spray with Pam.
- Pour a ball of batter onto the pan (keep the amount as much as you can flip easily) and add bacon.
- Once bubbles start forming near the center, or the edges start to brown, turn it over and cook for another minute or so.

Nutritional Info 2 Pancakes	
Fats	46g
Carbs	5g
Fiber	4g
Protein	12g

BACON-WRAPPED ASPARAGUS AND EGGS

Yield: 2 Servings

Requirements:

- 4 bacon slices
- 12 asparagus spears, divided
- 1 teaspoon minced garlic
- ½ teaspoon onion powder
- ½ teaspoon salt, divided
- ¼ teaspoon freshly ground black pepper, divided
- 1 tablespoon butter
- 4 eggs

Directions:

1.   Preheat your oven to 400°F.
2.   Make four bundles of 3 asparagus spears and wrap each with one slice of bacon. Put each bundle on a parchment-lined baking sheet.
3.   Spray the garlic, onion powder, ¼ teaspoon of salt, and a pinch of pepper over the bundles.
4.   Lay the tray in the preheated oven. Bake for 12 minutes, or until the bacon crisps.
5.   Melt the butter in a large skillet over medium-high heat. Carefully crack the eggs in pairs into the skillet, keeping the yolks unbroken.
6.   Cook the eggs to your desired doneness, about 5 minutes for a soft, semi-liquid egg.
7.   Sprinkle with the remaining ¼ teaspoon of salt and the remaining pepper.
8.   Take the asparagus out of the oven.
9.   Remove the eggs from the skillet, placing two eggs on top of two bundles of asparagus per serving.

Nutritional Info PER SERVING (2 EGGS WITH 2 BACON-WRAPPED ASPARAGUS BUNDLES)	
Fats	35.5g
Carbs	5g
Fiber	3.2g
Protein	33g

Steak and Eggs

Yield: 10 Servings, Serving size: 362 g

Requirements:

- 1 Onion (270 g)
- 1 Pepper (180 g)
- 4 Lbs Beef Chuck Shoulder
- 15 Eggs
- 120 g Heavy Cream
- 5 Oz Cheddar Cheese
- Salt, Pepper, Onion Powder, Garlic Powder to taste

Directions:

1. Chop up the peppers and onions
2. Fry the peppers and onions until translucent and set aside
3. Cook the steak on high for 3 minutes, flip and cook for 3 minutes more.
4. Let steak rest while cooking eggs.
5. Mix eggs, cream, and spices in a large bowl.
6. Cook in a non-stick pan, stirring occasionally until they are no longer runny.
7. Add cheese and stir some more.
8. Mix all the ingredients in a resealable container for breakfast!

Nutritional Info	
Fats	51g
Carbs	4g
Fiber	1g
Protein	45g

SCOTCH EGGS

Yield: Servings 2

Requirements:

- ½ cup breakfast sausage
- ½ teaspoon garlic powder
- ¼ teaspoon salt
- ⅛ teaspoon freshly ground black pepper
- 2 hardboiled eggs, peeled

Directions:

1. Preheat your oven to 400°F.
2. In a medium bowl, combine the sausage, garlic powder, salt, and pepper. Form the sausage into two balls.
3. On a piece of parchment paper, compress each ball into a ¼-inch-thick patty.
4. Lay one hardboiled egg in the center of each patty and carefully shape the sausage around the egg.
5. Lay the sausage-covered eggs on an ungreased baking sheet and into the preheated oven.
6. Bake for 25 minutes. Allow 5 minutes to cool, and then serve.

Nutritional Info (1 SAUSAGE-WRAPPED EGG)	
Fats	20.5g
Carbs	1g
Fiber	0g
Protein	16.7g

Spaghetti Squash Pancakes

Yield: 4 pancakes

Requirements:

- 4 Slices Thick Cut Bacon
- 2 Eggs
- 284g (10 Oz) Cooked Spaghetti Squash
- 1 teaspoon Garlic Powder
- 1 teaspoon Salt
- 1 teaspoon Pepper
- 1 teaspoon Onion Powder
- 30 g (1 Oz) Parmesan Cheese

Directions:

1. Cook the bacon until crunchy.
2. Combine eggs, Spaghetti Squash, spices and cheese in a bowl.
3. Crush the bacon and add to the mixture.
4. Heat some bacon grease in a skillet until shiny.
5. Pour the mixture into the bacon grease into four piles and use a spatula to squeeze the piles flat.
6. After the bottoms begin to brown, flip.
7. Serve as you like!!

Nutritional Info 2 pancakes	
Fats	18g
Carbs	10g
Fiber	2g
Protein	19g

CILANTRO CHILI CHICKEN SKEWERS

Yield: 4 Servings

Requirements:

- 1 cup fresh cilantro, chopped
- 2 tablespoons olive oil
- ¼ cup red chili paste
- 2 tablespoons soy sauce
- 2 garlic cloves, minced
- 1 teaspoon onion powder
- 1 teaspoon minced fresh ginger
- ¼ teaspoon freshly ground black pepper
- 1 pound boneless chicken thighs cut into 1-inch cubes
- 1 onion, roughly chopped
- 2 red bell peppers, roughly chopped

Directions:

1. Preheat your oven to broil.
2. In a large bowl, mix the cilantro, olive oil, red chili paste, soy sauce, garlic, onion powder, ginger, and black pepper.
3. Put in the thigh meat and turn until completely coated. Refrigerate for 15 minutes to marinate.
4. Take the chicken out of the refrigerator. Skewer the chicken cubes, with either onions or peppers between each piece.
5. Lay a foil-lined baking sheet on the lowest oven rack.
6. Place the chicken skewers directly on the middle rack above the baking sheet, vertical to the rack and cook for 3 minutes. Flip the skewers over and cook for 3 minutes more. Flip the skewers again, and cook for 4 minutes more.

7.   Using a meat thermometer, check the internal temperature. When it reaches 165°F, remove from the oven to cool. If you don't have a meat thermometer, feel free to use intuition.

8.   Serve on the skewers or remove the meat and vegetables from the skewers before adding to a plate.

Nutritional Info	
Fats	25g
Carbs	3g
Fiber	2g
Protein	22g

BEEF FAJITAS

Yield: 3 Servings

Requirements:

FOR THE RUB

- 1 teaspoon cumin
- ½ teaspoon chili powder
- ½ teaspoon garlic powder
- ½ teaspoon onion powder
- ¼ teaspoon paprika
- ¼ teaspoon salt
- ¼ teaspoon freshly ground black pepper

FOR THE STEAK

- 1 (1-pound) skirt steak
- 3 tablespoons olive oil, divided
- 1 red bell pepper, sliced
- 1 green bell pepper, sliced
- 1 jalapeño pepper, sliced
- 1 serrano pepper, minced
- 1 onion, sliced
- 2 garlic cloves, minced
- 2 tablespoons fresh cilantro, chopped
- 1 lime, quartered
- 3 low-carb tortillas (optional)

Directions:

To make the rub

1.   In a large bowl, combine the cumin, chili powder, garlic powder, onion powder, paprika, salt, and pepper.

To make the steak

1.   Cover the steak with the rub, massaging it thoroughly into the meat. Set aside.
2.   In a large skillet over medium-high heat, heat 1 tablespoon of olive oil for 1 minute. Add the red peppers, green peppers, jalapeño peppers, serrano peppers, onions, and garlic and sauté for 6 to 7 minutes, until browned and soft. Pour the pepper and onion mixture to a bowl and set aside.
3.   Put 1 more tablespoon of olive oil into the skillet. Heat on medium-high for 1 minute. Lay the seasoned steak into the pan and cook it for 3 to 4 minutes per side for medium-rare. Take the steak out of the skillet. Set aside and let it rest for at least 3 minutes.
4.   Put the remaining tablespoon of olive oil into the skillet. Heat on medium- high heat for 1 minute. Put the peppers and onions back into the skillet and sauté for 2 minutes. Chop the steak into ¼-inch-thick strips and add them to the skillet with the peppers and cook for 2 to 3 minutes until browned.
5.   Add the chopped cilantro. Remove from the heat and serve as you like!!

Nutritional Info PER SERVING (1 FAJITA)	
Fats	52.5g
Carbs	15.9g
Fiber	2.1g
Protein	57g

AVOCADO CHICKEN BURGER

Yield: Servings 4

Requirements:

- 1 pound ground chicken
- ½ cup almond flour
- 2 garlic cloves, minced
- 1 teaspoon onion powder
- ¼ teaspoon salt
- ⅛ teaspoon freshly ground black pepper
- 1 avocado, diced
- 2 tablespoons olive oil
- 4 low-carb buns or lettuce wraps (optional)

Directions:

1. In a large bowl, combine the ground chicken, almond flour, garlic, onion powder, salt, and pepper.
2. Add the avocado, carefully incorporating into the meat while forming four patties. Set aside.
3. In a large skillet over medium heat, heat the olive oil for about 1 minute.
4. Place the patties into the skillet and cook for about 8 minutes per side.
5. Serve as you like.

Nutritional Info PER SERVING (1 PATTY)	
Fats	25.7g
Carbs	2.9g
Fiber	5g
Protein	33.9g

POT ROAST WITH TURNIPS AND RADISHES

Yield: 6 Servings

Requirements:

- 1 (4- to 5-pound) bottom round rump roast
- ¾ teaspoon salt
- ½ teaspoon freshly ground black pepper
- 3 tablespoons olive oil
- 1 onion, quartered
- 3 cups beef stock, divided
- 2 garlic cloves
- 2 fresh thyme sprigs
- 2 turnips, peeled, roughly chopped
- 2 cups radishes, halved
- ¼ cup heavy (whipping) cream

Directions:

1. Preheat your oven to 475°F.
2. Sprinkle with the salt and pepper to taste.
3. In a large Dutch oven over medium-high heat, heat the olive oil for 1 minute. Put the roast into the pot. Brown on all sides, about 3 minutes per side, and set aside.
4. Add the onion to the pot and brown for about 3 minutes, stirring. Take the onion out of the pot and set them aside with the roast.
5. Pour ½ cup of beef stock into the pot, scraping the bottom of the pan to release any browned bits.
6. Put the residual 2½ cups of beef stock, the garlic, and thyme into the pot and mix well.
7. Place the roast and onion back into the pot. Put the turnips and radishes in the pot, surrounding the roast.

8. Lay the pot, uncovered, into the preheated oven. Instantly reduce the heat to 400°F and cook for 6 to 6½ hours, or until the internal temperature of the meat reaches 130°F. Take the roast out of the oven and allow it to cool for 2 to 3 minutes. Transfer the roast and vegetables to a dish.

9. Into a large saucepan over medium-high heat, pour the remaining liquid from the Dutch oven. Put in the heavy cream. Bring the liquid to a boil and reduce the heat to medium and let the sauce reduce for 4 to 5 minutes.

10. Chop the pot roast and serve with the reduced sauce and vegetables.

Nutritional Info	
Fats	25.2g
Carbs	3.9g
Fiber	1.7g
Protein	69g

CURRIED CHICKEN

Yield: 4 Servings

Requirements:

- 4 tablespoons coconut oil
- ¼ cup diced onion
- 1 cup bamboo shoots
- 1 pound boneless chicken thighs, diced
- 1 teaspoon minced fresh ginger
- 1 tablespoon curry powder
- 1 tablespoon paprika
- 1¼ cups coconut milk
- ¼ cup heavy (whipping) cream
- ¼ teaspoon salt
- ⅛ teaspoon freshly ground black pepper

Directions:

1. Heat the coconut oil for about 1 minute in a large skillet over medium-high heat and add the onion, bamboo shoots, and chicken meat and cook for 5 minutes.
2. Mix in the ginger, curry powder, and paprika and continue cooking for 2 to 3 minutes more.
3. Add the coconut milk and heavy cream. Reduce the heat to medium-low.
4. Simmer for about 15 minutes and sprinkle with salt and pepper to taste.
5. Serve over Cauliflower Rice.

Nutritional Info	
Fats	52g
Carbs	5.3g
Fiber	3.9g
Protein	23.5g

BEEF STROGANOFF

Yield: 4 Servings

Requirements:

- 1 (1-pound) beef roast
- ¼ teaspoon salt
- ¼ teaspoon freshly ground black pepper
- 1 tablespoon olive oil
- ½ cup diced onion
- 1 cup chopped mushrooms
- 1 teaspoon minced garlic
- 4 cups sliced cabbage
- 1½ cups beef broth
- ½ cup heavy (whipping) cream
- ½ cream cheese, at room temperature
- 1 teaspoon tomato paste

Directions:

1. Sprinkle the roast with the salt and pepper and set aside.
2. Heat the olive oil for about 1 minute in a large skillet over medium-high heat and add the roast to the skillet. Brown on all sides for around 2 minutes on each side.
3. Take the roast out of the skillet, preserving any juices, and set aside.
4. Add the onion, mushrooms, and garlic to the skillet and cook for 2 minutes, or until tender.
5. In a large slow cooker, layer the cabbage on the bottom. Top with the roast.
6. Transfer the onion mixture to the cooker.
7. In a large bowl, mix together the beef broth, heavy cream, cream cheese,
8. and tomato paste. Add to the slower cooker and cover.

9. Cook the roast on low for about 7 hours.
10. With a fork or tongs, shred the roast. Serve with the cabbage.

Nutritional Info	
Fats	27g
Carbs	5.8g
Fiber	2.3g
Protein	40.4g

JAMAICAN JERK CHICKEN

Yield: 4 Servings

Requirements:

- 1 onion, finely chopped
- ½ cup finely chopped scallions
- 3 tablespoons soy sauce
- 1 tablespoon apple cider vinegar
- 1 tablespoon olive oil
- 2 teaspoons chopped fresh thyme
- 2 teaspoons Splenda, or other sugar substitute
- 1 teaspoon liquid smoke
- 1 teaspoon salt
- 1 teaspoon allspice
- 1 teaspoon cayenne pepper
- 1 teaspoon freshly ground black pepper
- ½ teaspoon nutmeg
- ½ teaspoon cinnamon
- 1 whole chicken, quartered

Directions:

1.   Combine the onion, scallion, soy sauce, cider vinegar, olive oil, thyme, Splenda, liquid smoke, salt, allspice, cayenne pepper, black pepper, nutmeg, and cinnamon in a medium bowl and mix.

2.   Put the chicken pieces skin-side down In a large dish and pour the marinade over it. Marinate covered, in the refrigerator, for at least 4 hours.

3.   When you want to start cooking, preheat your oven to 425°F.

4.   Lay the baking dish with the chicken into the preheated oven and cook for 30 minutes.

5.   Take the baking dish out of the oven and turn the chicken skin-side up.

6. Place the pan back into the oven and cook for 20 to 30 minutes more.
7. Cool the chicken for 5 minutes.
8. Cut and Serve.

Nutritional Info	
Fats	36g
Carbs	3.1g
Fiber	0.9g
Protein	42.8g

FIVE-ALARM BEEF CHILI

Yield: 12 Servings

Requirements:

FOR THE CHILI

- 3 tablespoons olive oil
- 2 cups diced onion
- 5 garlic cloves, minced
- 2 green bell peppers, diced
- 2 poblano peppers, diced
- 3 serrano peppers, minced
- 3 jalapeño peppers, diced
- 2 to 3 habanero peppers, minced (adjust for heat level; optional)
- 3 pounds 80 percent lean ground beef
- 1 cup tomato paste
- 2¼ cups crushed tomatoes
- 1½ cups diced tomatoes
- 2 cups dark beer
- 1½ tablespoons dark chili powder
- ½ teaspoon paprika
- 1 teaspoon salt
- 1 teaspoon freshly ground black pepper
- ½ teaspoon cumin

FOR THE TOPPINGS

- 2 cups shredded Cheddar cheese
- 1 cup sour cream
- Chopped fresh cilantro, for garnish (optional)

Directions:

To make the chili

1. Heat the olive oil for 1 minute in a large stockpot over medium heat and add the onion and garlic and cook for 3 minutes until tender.
2. Put the bell peppers, poblano peppers, serrano peppers, jalapeño peppers, and habanero peppers (if using) into the pot and mix well and cook for 3 to 4 minutes.
3. Put the ground beef in the peppers and onions. Crush with the back of a spoon while browning for 4 minutes.
4. Put the tomato paste, crushed tomatoes, and diced tomatoes into the pot and mix thoroughly.
5. Put the beer in and raise the heat to high and bring the mixture to a boil.
6. Once the chili boils, cover and reduce the heat to medium-low and cook for 1½ hours.
7. Put in the chili powder, paprika, salt, pepper, and cumin and stir to mix.
8. Cook for 5 more minutes while stirring a little.
9. Serve the chili with the shredded cheese and sour cream. Sprinkle cilantro on top if you wish.

Nutritional Info	
Fats	34g
Carbs	11g
Fiber	4g
Protein	39g

BARBECUE ONION AND GOAT CHEESE FLATBREAD

Yield: 2 Servings

Requirements:

FOR THE FLATBREAD

- 2 tablespoons coconut flour
- ⅛ teaspoon baking powder
- 4 egg whites
- ¼ teaspoon onion powder
- ¼ teaspoon garlic powder
- ¼ cup coconut milk

FOR THE TOPPINGS

- 2 tablespoons sugar-free barbecue sauce
- ¾ cup goat cheese, crumbled
- ½ cup sliced yellow onion
- ½ teaspoon minced garlic
- ⅛ teaspoon freshly ground black pepper

Directions:

To make the flatbread

1. Thoroughly mix the coconut flour, baking powder, egg whites, onion powder, garlic powder, and coconut milk in a medium bowl, until there are no lumps.

2. Heat a large skillet over medium-high heat. Pour the coconut batter into the skillet and turn the pan so the batter covers the entire pan and cook for 2 minutes, or until the edges brown. Flip and cook for 1 to 2 minutes more.

3.   Take the flatbread out of the pan.

To assemble the pizza

1.   Preheat your oven to 425°F.
2.   Pour the barbecue sauce, goat cheese, onion, garlic, and pepper on top of the cooked flatbread. Lay the flatbread on a baking sheet and place it in the preheated oven. Bake for 5 to 7 minutes, or until the cheese melts.
3.   Take it out of the oven and cool the flatbread for 2 minutes before slicing and serving.

Nutritional Info (½ FLATBREAD PIZZA)	
Fats	39g
Carbs	13g
Fiber	4g
Protein	36g

SESAME BROILED CHICKEN THIGHS

Yield: 4 Servings

Requirements:

- 4 bone-in, skin-on chicken thighs
- ¼ teaspoon salt
- ¼ teaspoon freshly ground black pepper
- 2 tablespoons soy sauce
- 2 tablespoons sugar-free maple syrup
- 1 tablespoon sesame oil
- 1 teaspoon minced garlic
- 1 teaspoon red wine vinegar
- ½ teaspoon crushed red pepper flakes

Directions:

1. Sprinkle the chicken with the salt and pepper and set aside.
2. In a bowl large enough to hold the chicken, mix the soy sauce, maple syrup, sesame oil, garlic, vinegar, and red pepper flakes. Preserve about one-fourth of the sauce.
3. Place the chicken thighs in the bowl, skin-side up and dip in the soy sauce. Refrigerate to marinate for at least 15 minutes.
4. Preheat your oven to broil.
5. Take the chicken out of the refrigerator. Lay the thighs skin-side down in the baking dish.
6. Put the dish in the preheated oven, about six inches from the broiler.
7. Broil for 5 to 6 minutes with the oven door slightly open. Flip the chicken skin- side up and broil for about 2 minutes more.
8. Flip the chicken again so it is now skin-side down. Shift the baking dish to the bottom rack of the oven. Close the oven door and broil for an additional 6 to 8 minutes.

9. Flip the chicken again to skin-side up and baste with the reserved sauce.
10. Close the oven door and broil for 2 more minutes.
11. Take the chicken out of the oven. check the internal temperature of the meat with a meat thermometer. It should reach at least 165°F.
12. Cool the chicken for 5 minutes before serving.

Nutritional Info (1 THIGH)	
Fats	26g
Carbs	2.2g
Fiber	0g
Protein	27.1g

GROUND BEEF TACO SALAD

Yield: 4 Servings

Requirements:

FOR THE TACO MEAT

- 2 tablespoons olive oil
- ½ cup diced onion
- 2 garlic cloves, minced
- 1 green bell pepper, diced
- 1 jalapeño pepper, diced
- 6 ounces diced tomatoes, divided
- 1 pound 80-percent lean ground beef
- ½ teaspoon cumin
- ½ teaspoon paprika
- ¼ teaspoon salt
- ¼ teaspoon freshly ground black pepper
- 1 avocado, diced

FOR THE TOPPINGS

- ½ cup shredded Cheddar cheese
- ¼ cup sour cream
- Fresh cilantro, chopped
- To make the taco meat

Directions:

1.   Heat the olive oil in a large skillet over medium-high heat, for about 1 minute. Put in the onion and garlic and cook for 2 minutes, until tender.

2.   Put the bell pepper, jalapeño pepper, and 3 ounces of diced tomatoes into the skillet and cook for 3 to 4 more minutes.

3. Pour the mixture into a large bowl and set aside. Preserve any liquid left in the skillet and place back over the heat.
4. Put the ground beef into the skillet and cook for 8 to 10 minutes, crumbling the meat, until browned.
5. Put in the cumin, paprika, salt, and pepper and stir to combine.
6. Transfer the beef to the large bowl with the onion and pepper mixture. Toss to combine.
7. Add the remaining 3 ounces of tomatoes and mix.
8. Carefully stir in the avocado. Do not overmix.
9. Plate each serving of taco salad with a portion of the Cheddar cheese, sour cream, and cilantro toppings.

Nutritional Info	
Fats	44.5g
Carbs	10.9g
Fiber	5.8g
Protein	36.6g

BACON RANCH CHEESY CHICKEN BREASTS

Yield: 4 Servings

Requirements:

- Cooking spray for the baking dish
- 3 tablespoons olive oil
- 4 boneless chicken breasts
- ½ teaspoon salt
- ¼ teaspoon freshly ground black pepper
- 1 tablespoon garlic powder
- 8 bacon slices
- 4 tablespoons butter
- 4 tablespoons Ranch Dressing , or purchased bottled dressing
- ½ cup shredded Cheddar cheese, divided
- ½ cup shredded mozzarella cheese
- ½ cup grated Parmesan cheese
- ½ teaspoon dried parsley

Directions:

1. Preheat your oven to 350°F and prepare a baking dish with cooking spray.
2. Heat the olive oil for about 1 minute in a large skillet over medium-high heat. Sprinkle the chicken breasts with the salt, pepper, and garlic powder. Put them into the skillet. Heat each breast for 5 minutes per side.
3. Chop the bacon into small pieces, about 12 cuts per slice.
4. Lay the chicken into the prepared dish. Spread 1 tablespoon of butter and 1 tablespoon of ranch dressing over each breast.
5. Place the bacon on top of the chicken, covering each breast completely.
6. Put the dish in the preheated oven and bake for 30 minutes. Take out of the oven.

7. Sprinkle equal amounts of the Cheddar, mozzarella, and Parmesan cheeses over the bacon-topped breasts. Season with the dried parsley. Place the dish back into the oven.

8. Bake for another 10 to 12 minutes, or until the cheese melts.

9. Take the dish out of the oven and allow to rest for about 2 minutes before serving.

Nutritional Info	
Fats	52.3g
Carbs	4.2g
Fiber	0.3g
Protein	46.5g

PHILLY CHEESESTEAK STUFFED PEPPERS

Yield: 3 Servings

Requirements:

- 4 green bell peppers, seeded, tops reserved, plus ¼ cup thinly sliced green bell pepper from reserved tops
- 3 tablespoons butter
- ¼ cup chopped onion
- 1 pound shaved beefsteak
- 1 garlic clove, minced
- 1 teaspoon salt
- 1 teaspoon freshly ground black pepper
- ½ teaspoon paprika
- ½ teaspoon ground coriander
- ¼ teaspoon dill
- ¼ teaspoon crushed red pepper flakes
- ½ teaspoon garlic powder
- ½ teaspoon onion powder
- 8 slices pepper Jack cheese, divided
- 2½ tablespoons mayonnaise

Directions:

1. Preheat your oven to 400°F.
2. Chop off a thin piece from the bottom of each whole bell pepper so it will not tip over. Lay the 4 peppers on a baking sheet and into the preheated oven. Bake for 10 to 15 minutes.
3. Heat the butter In a large skillet over medium-high heat for 1 minute. Put in the onions and sliced green bell peppers and cook for 3 minutes.
4. Put in the steak, garlic, salt, black pepper, paprika, coriander, dill, red pepper flakes, garlic powder, and onion powder and cook for 6 to 7 minutes

until the meat browns completely, breaking up the meat as it cooks. Reduce the heat to medium- low.

5.   Take the whole bell peppers out of the oven and place 1 slice of pepper Jack cheese in each pepper.

6.   Transfer the steak mixture to a medium bowl and continue to shred the meat. Put in the mayonnaise and mix well to combine.

7.   Stuff each pepper with an equal amount of the meat mixture. Top each pepper with 1 of the left over 4 cheese slices.

8.   Put the stuffed peppers back in the oven and cook for 5 to 7 minutes, or until the cheese melts.

9.   Take out of the oven and serve right away.

Nutritional Info PER SERVING (1 STUFFED PEPPER)	
Fats	42.5g
Carbs	11.7g
Fiber	3.1g
Protein	38.2g

CHICKEN FAJITA STUFFED BELL PEPPERS

Yield: 6 Servings

Requirements:

- ½ cup butter, divided
- 1 pound boneless chicken thighs
- ½ cup chopped onion
- 1½ cups Cauliflower "Rice"
- ¼ cup chopped scallions
- ½ cup chicken broth
- 2 teaspoons chili powder
- 1 teaspoon paprika
- 1 teaspoon salt
- ½ teaspoon cumin
- ½ teaspoon garlic powder
- ¼ teaspoon dried oregano
- ¼ teaspoon cayenne pepper (optional)
- 6 bell peppers, tops removed and seeded
- 1 cup shredded Mexican cheese blend

Directions:

1. Preheat your oven to 350°F.
2. Heat 6 tablespoons of butter In a large skillet over medium-high heat. Put in the chicken. Cook for 3 to 4 minutes on each side. Cover. Lower the heat to medium-low and cook for another 10 to 12 minutes. Check the chicken for doneness. Set aside to cool if done.
3. Once cooled, cut up the chicken into small pieces. Set aside.
4. In a large skillet over medium-high heat, melt the remaining 2 tablespoons of butter. Put in the onion and cook for 3 to 4 minutes, until translucent.

5.   Add the Cauliflower "Rice" , shredded chicken, scallions, chicken broth, chili powder, paprika, salt, cumin, garlic powder, dried oregano, and cayenne pepper (if using).
6.   Chop off a thin piece from the bottom of each bell pepper so it will not tip over.
7.   Lay the peppers open-side up on a baking sheet.
8.   Fill each bell pepper with the same amount of the chicken mixture.
9.   Top evenly with the Mexican cheese blend.
10. Put the sheet in the oven. Bake for about 30 minutes, or until the cheese browns.

Nutritional Info PER SERVING (1 PEPPER)	
Fats	28.3g
Carbs	7.8g
Fiber	4g
Protein	29.2g

Week 3 Diet Plan

	Breakfast	Lunch	Dinner
M O N	EGGS BENEDICT (Pg 98)	BUFFALO CHICKEN WINGS (Pg 110)	ALMOND BUTTER BREAD (Pg 124)
T U E	Western Scrambled Eggs (Pg 100)	GRILLED HANGER STEAK WITH CILANTRO CREMA (Pg 112)	BACON-WRAPPED SCALLOPS AND BROCCOLINI (Pg 126)
W E D	DENVER OMELET (Pg 102)	CILANTRO LIME SHRIMP AND VEGETABLE KEBABS (Pg 114)	COCONUT ALMOND FLOUR BREAD (Pg 128)
T H U	Bacon Hash (Pg 104)	CAULIFLOWER PIZZA (Pg 116)	BACON-WRAPPED JALAPEÑO CHICKEN (Pg 130)
F R I	PORTOBELLO, SAUSAGE, AND CHEESE (Pg 105)	GREEN-CHILE CHICKEN ENCHILADA CASSEROLE (Pg 118)	CRAB CAKES WITH GARLIC AIOLI (Pg 132)
S A T	Keto Breakfast Pizza (Pg 107)	DOUBLE BACON CHEESEBURGER (Pg 120)	CHEESY TACO SHELLS (Pg 135)
S U N	ALMOND FLOUR PANCAKES (Pg 108)	SHRIMP, BAMBOO SHOOT, AND BROCCOLI STIR-FRY (Pg 122)	PARMESAN-CRUSTED TILAPIA WITH SAUTÉED (Pg 137)

Week 3 Cookbook

EGGS BENEDICT

Yield: Servings 2

Requirements:

FOR THE HOLLANDAISE SAUCE

- 2 eggs
- 1½ teaspoons freshly squeezed lemon juice
- ¼ cup butter, melted
- ¼ teaspoon salt

FOR THE EGGS

- 4 slices bacon
- 1 teaspoon vinegar
- 4 eggs

Directions:

To make the hollandaise sauce

1. In a large heat-safe bowl, vigorously mix two eggs and the lemon juice together until thick and roughly double in volume.
2. Fill a large skillet with 1 inch of water and heat to simmering. Lower the heat to medium.
3. Wear a heat-resistant oven glove and hold the bowl with the eggs over the water, making sure it does not touch the water. Stir the mixture for about 3 minutes, being careful not to scramble the eggs.
4. Gradually add the butter to the egg mixture and carry on stirring until it thickens, about 2 minutes.
5. Add salt to taste and stir more.
6. Refrigerate the sauce until cool.

To make the eggs

1. Pour the water out of the skillet and place it over medium-high heat. Lay the bacon in the skillet and cook for 3 minutes per side. Transfer the bacon to paper towels to drain.
2. In a medium saucepan half full of water, pour the vinegar and bring to a low boil.
3. Cautiously crack the eggs into the water, being careful not to break the yolks.
4. Lower the heat to medium-low and cook for 3 to 4 minutes.
5. Take the eggs out. Allow them to drain and set aside.

To assemble the finished dish

6. Cut each bacon slice in half. Lay two halves on a plate and top with one egg. Do again with 2 more halves and another egg.
7. Pour hollandaise sauce all over.
8. Do again with the remaining bacon and eggs for the second serving.

Nutritional Info PER SERVING (2 EGGS, 2 BACON SLICES, ½ OF THE HOLLANDAISE SAUCE)	
Fats	54g
Carbs	1.8g
Fiber	0g
Protein	32.6g

Western Scrambled Eggs

Yield: 10 Servings

Requirements:

- 10 Eggs
- 120 mL Heavy Cream
- 100 mL Water
- Salt, Pepper, Onion Powder, Garlic Powder to taste
- 225g Diced Ham
- 113g Green Onions
- 234g Diced Tomatoes, drained
- 8 Oz Cheddar Cheese

Directions:

1. Preheat your oven to 450 degrees.
2. Combine Eggs, Cream, Water, and Spices.
3. Spray a large cookie sheet and put in the eggs.
4. Cook for 8 minutes.
5. Add toppings.
6. Cook for 2 more minutes or until the cheese melts.
7. Let it cool for 5 minutes.
8. Scramble the mixture and divide into breakfast portions.

Nutritional Info	
Fats	16g
Carbs	3g
Fiber	1g
Protein	14g

DENVER OMELET

Yield: 1 Serving

Requirements:

- 1 tablespoon butter
- ¼ cup chopped onion
- ¼ cup chopped red bell pepper
- ¼ cup chopped green bell pepper
- ½ teaspoon minced garlic
- ¼ cup diced cooked ham
- 2 eggs, beaten
- ¼ teaspoon salt
- ⅛ teaspoon freshly ground black pepper
- ¼ cup shredded Cheddar cheese

Directions:

1. In a medium nonstick skillet over medium-high heat, melt the butter.
2. Put in the onion, red bell pepper, green bell pepper, garlic, and ham. Sauté until the ham is crisp, about 2 minutes.
3. In a small bowl, beat the eggs and sprinkle with the salt and pepper. Put the eggs into the skillet with the vegetables and ham. Reduce the heat to medium.
4. Cook the eggs for 3 to 4 minutes. Turn the omelet over. After turning, top one-half of the omelet with the Cheddar cheese.
5. After 1 to 2 minutes, fold the omelet over, wrapping the cheese and cook for another 1 to 2 minutes, until the cheese is melted.
6. Take the omelet out of the skillet to a plate, and serve.

Nutritional Info PER SERVING (1 OMELET)	
Fats	32.7g
Carbs	7g
Fiber	2.2g
Protein	24.7g

Bacon Hash

Yield: 2 Servings (2 eggs each)

Requirements:

- 1 Small Pepper (159 g)
- 1 Small Onion (101 g)
- Several slices of Jalapenos
- 6 Slices Bacon
- 4 Eggs

Directions:

1. Chop the pepper and onions into thin strips.
2. Chop the jalapeno slices as small as possible.
3. Fry the vegetables in a cast iron pan.
4. Take the veggies out when they are translucent and browning.
5. Process the bacon in a food processor until it gets broken into chunks. Don't let it become a paste.
6. Combine all the ingredients together.
7. Cook the hash until the bacon is slightly crisp.
8. Place on a plate and top with a fried egg!

Nutritional Info	
Fats	24g
Carbs	11g
Fiber	2g
Protein	23g

PORTOBELLO, SAUSAGE, AND CHEESE BREAKFAST "BURGER"

Yield: 1 Serving

Requirements:

- 1 tablespoon olive oil
- 2 Portobello mushroom caps, stemmed, gills removed
- ¼ cup breakfast sausage
- 2 (2-ounce) slices American cheese

Directions:

1. Heat the olive oil for 1 minute in a medium nonstick skillet over medium heat,.
2. Put the mushroom caps into the hot oil, cap side up and cook for about 5 minutes per side, or until browned.
3. Heat one more medium skillet over medium-high heat.
4. Make the breakfast sausage into a ½-inch-thick patty. Put it in the center of the heated pan and cook for 4 to 5 minutes. Turn and cook 2 to 3 minutes more.
5. When the sausage is nearly done, lower the heat to low. Top the patty with the American cheese and cook until the cheese melts.
6. Take the mushroom caps out of the skillet and place on a plate.
7. Put the cheese-topped patty on one mushroom cap. Top with the remaining mushroom cap and serve.

Nutritional Info 1 Burger	
Fats	41g
Carbs	7g
Fiber	3g
Protein	24g

Keto Breakfast Pizza

Yield: 2 Servings

Requirements:

- 4 Eggs
- 4 Slices Bacon
- 2 Oz. Cheddar Cheese
- 10 Slices Pepperoni
- Salt, Pepper, Garlic Powder and Onion Powder to taste

Directions:

1. Cook the bacon and preserve the bacon grease in the skillet.
2. Allow the pan to cool a little.
3. Crack four eggs into the pan, try to put them close together.
4. Season.
5. Cook in the oven at 450 for 6 minutes.
6. Put in the cheddar and toppings.
7. Cook for 4 more minutes.
8. Place the bacon on top and serve.

Nutritional Info	
Fats	24g
Carbs	1g
Fiber	0g
Protein	22g

ALMOND FLOUR PANCAKES

Yield: 3 Servings (6 pancakes)

Requirements:

- 1 cup almond flour
- 1 tablespoon stevia, or other sugar substitute
- ¼ teaspoon salt
- 1 teaspoon baking powder
- 2 eggs
- ⅛ cup heavy (whipping) cream
- ⅛ cup sparkling water
- ½ teaspoon pure vanilla extract
- 2 tablespoons coconut oil, melted
- Cooking spray for griddle

Directions:

1. Preheat a griddle over medium-high heat.
2. In a large bowl, combine the almond flour, stevia, salt, and baking powder.
3. Create a small well in the center of the dry ingredients and put in the eggs, heavy cream, sparkling water, vanilla, and coconut oil. Mix well.
4. Sprinkle the griddle with cooking spray. Pour the batter onto the griddle in desired amounts and cook the pancakes for 2 to 3 minutes, until you see little bubbles, then turn and cook for an additional 1 to 2 minutes.
5. Take the pancakes out of the griddle when done. Do again with the remaining batter.

Nutritional Info (2 pancakes)	
Fats	34g
Carbs	4g
Fiber	4g
Protein	3.8g

BUFFALO CHICKEN WINGS

Yield: 4 Servings

Requirements:

- 1 tablespoon olive oil
- 1 teaspoon salt, divided
- ½ teaspoon freshly ground black pepper, divided
- 2 pounds chicken wings
- ¼ cup hot sauce
- 1 tablespoon butter, melted
- ¼ teaspoon cayenne pepper
- 1 cup Bleu Cheese Sauce or Ranch Dressing , or purchased bottled dressing

Directions:

1. Preheat your oven to 400°F.
2. In a large bowl, combine the olive oil, ½ teaspoon of salt, and ¼ teaspoon of black pepper. Put in the wings and stir to coat.
3. Equally divide the wings between two baking sheets. Place the sheets in the oven. Bake for 45 to 50 minutes, or until the outer skin is crispy.
4. In another large bowl, combine the hot sauce, butter, cayenne pepper, the remaining ½ teaspoon of salt, and remaining ¼ teaspoon of black pepper.
5. Put in the cooked wings. Toss them in the sauce for 1 minute to coat.
6. Serve with Bleu Cheese Sauce or Ranch Dressing .

Nutritional Info	
Fats	23.4g
Carbs	3.7g
Fiber	0g
Protein	66.5g

GRILLED HANGER STEAK WITH CILANTRO CREMA

Yield: 3 Servings

Requirements:

FOR THE CILANTRO CREMA

- ¼ cup sliced scallions
- ¼ cup fresh cilantro, chopped
- 1 garlic clove
- 1 teaspoon grated lime rind
- 1½ teaspoons freshly squeezed lime juice
- 3 tablespoons mayonnaise
- 3 tablespoons sour cream
- ¼ teaspoon salt

FOR THE RUB

- 1 teaspoon onion powder
- ¾ teaspoon salt
- ½ teaspoon freshly ground black pepper
- ½ teaspoon garlic powder
- ¼ teaspoon cumin
- ¼ teaspoon paprika
- ⅛ teaspoon ginger

FOR THE STEAK

- 1 (1- to 1½-pound) hanger steak
- 4 tablespoons butter

Directions:

To make the cilantro crema

1. In a food processor, combine the scallions, cilantro, garlic, lime rind, and lime juice. Pulse until the scallions and cilantro blend.
2. Put in the mayonnaise, sour cream, and salt. Pulse until completely mixed.
3. Refrigerate until ready to serve.

To make the rub

1. In a small bowl, combine the onion powder, salt, pepper, garlic powder, cumin, paprika, and ginger.

To make the steak

1. Abundantly coat the steak with the rub and set aside.
2. In a large skillet over medium high heat, heat the butter for about 2 minutes, being cautious not to burn it.
3. Put the seasoned steak into the skillet. Cook for 3 minutes on each side for rare; 4 minutes per side for medium-rare.
4. Take the steak out of the pan and tent with aluminum foil. Let the steak cool for 7 to 10 minutes before chopping.
5. Serve the sliced steak with the cilantro crema on the side.

Nutritional Info	
Fats	51.3g
Carbs	8g
Fiber	1g
Protein	43g

CILANTRO LIME SHRIMP AND VEGETABLE KEBABS WITH CHIPOTLE SOUR CREAM SAUCE

Yield: 2 Servings

Requirements:

FOR THE SHRIMP

- ¾ pound shrimp, peeled and deveined
- 2 tablespoons olive oil
- 2 tablespoons freshly squeezed lime juice
- ½ teaspoon garlic powder, divided
- ½ teaspoon onion powder, divided
- ¼ cup chopped fresh cilantro
- ¼ teaspoon salt
- ¼ teaspoon freshly ground black pepper
- ½ teaspoon liquid smoke (optional)
- ½ cup roughly chopped bell pepper
- ⅓ cup roughly chopped onion

FOR THE CHIPOTLE SOUR CREAM SAUCE

- ¼ cup sour cream
- 1 teaspoon chipotle pepper powder

Directions:

To make the shrimp

1. Heat a grill, or griddle, to medium-high heat.
2. In a large bowl, Mix together the shrimp, olive oil, lime juice, ¼ teaspoon garlic powder, ¼ teaspoon onion powder, cilantro, salt, and pepper. If cooking indoors, add the liquid smoke (if using).

3. Mix until the shrimp are coated completely.

To make the chipotle sour cream sauce

1. In a small bowl, combine the sour cream, chipotle powder, the remaining ¼ teaspoon garlic powder, and the remaining ¼ teaspoon onion powder.
2. Refrigerate until ready to serve.

To make the kebabs

1. Skewer the shrimp, alternating with the bell peppers and onions.
2. Put the kebabs on the preheated grill and cook for 3 to 5 minutes. Turn, and cook for 3 to 5 minutes more.
3. Take them off the grill. Check the shrimp for doneness. The shrimp is done when firm in texture, opaque, and tinged with its signature pink-orange color.
4. Take the shrimp and vegetables off the kebabs. Serve with the chipotle sour cream sauce.

Nutritional Info	
Fats	23g
Carbs	8.7g
Fiber	1.2g
Protein	40.3g

CAULIFLOWER PIZZA

Yield: 2 Servings

Requirements:

FOR THE CRUST

- ¾ teaspoon salt, divided
- 2 cups cauliflower florets
- 1 egg
- 2½ cups shredded mozzarella cheese, divided
- ½ teaspoon garlic powder
- ⅛ teaspoon freshly ground black pepper

FOR THE PIZZA

- ¼ cup sugar-free pizza sauce, divided
- 10 pepperoni slices, divided

Directions:

To make the crust

1. Preheat your oven to 450°F.
2. Bring a large pot of water to a boil. Sprinkle with ½ teaspoon of salt.
3. Cautiously put the cauliflower into the boiling water and cook for 8 minutes. Drain completely, using paper towels to soak up any excess moisture.
4. Put the drained cauliflower into a food processor. Pulse for 1 minute until the cauliflower is "riced."
5. Place the cauliflower in a large bowl and add the egg, 1 cup of mozzarella cheese, the garlic powder, the remaining ¼ teaspoon of salt, and pepper. Stir until the cheese fully melts.
6. Divide the cauliflower dough into two equal balls.

7. On a parchment-lined baking sheet, spread every ball into an 8-inch crust.
8. The crust should be very slim.
9. Lay the crusts in the preheated oven. Bake for 15 to 20 minutes, or until browned. The edges of the crust should be nearly burned.
10. Take the crusts out of the oven. Turn the oven to broil.

To make the pizza

1. Spread ⅛ cup of pizza sauce over each crust.
2. Top each crust with ¾ cup of mozzarella cheese and half the pepperoni.
3. Place the sheet back into the oven. Bake the pizzas for 2 to 3 minutes, or until the cheese is melted and bubbling.
4. Take the sheet out of the oven and allow the pizzas to cool for 3 to 5 minutes before slicing and serving.

Nutritional Info	
Fats	31g
Carbs	8.6g
Fiber	2.3g
Protein	35.5g

GREEN-CHILE CHICKEN ENCHILADA CASSEROLE

Yield: 8 Servings

Requirements:

- 3 cups chicken broth
- 1½ pounds boneless chicken thighs
- 2 cups chopped fresh roasted green chiles, or canned
- 1 cup sour cream
- 2 cups shredded Monterey Jack cheese
- ½ cup diced onion
- 1 tablespoon minced garlic
- ½ teaspoon salt
- ½ teaspoon freshly ground black pepper
- ¼ teaspoon cayenne pepper
- 1 tablespoon olive oil
- 1 bunch fresh cilantro, chopped
- 2 low-carb tortillas cut into ½-inch-wide strips

Directions:

1. Preheat your oven to 400°F.
2. Pour the chicken broth into a large pot over high heat and bring to a boil.
3. Lower the heat to a simmer. Add the chicken thighs and cook for 12 minutes.
4. Take the thighs out and set aside to cool. Once cooled, shred the chicken into bite-size pieces. Place in a large bowl.
5. Add the green chiles, sour cream, Monterey Jack cheese, onion, garlic, salt, black pepper, and cayenne pepper yo the shredded chicken and mix well.

6. In a medium skillet over medium-high heat, heat the olive oil for 1 minute.
7. Put in the tortilla strips and crisp for 2 to 3 minutes. Stir to avoid burning.
8. Pour the chicken mixture into a large baking dish. Apply the cilantro abundantly to the top of the chicken mixture, then put in the tortilla strips.
9. Put the dish in the preheated oven and cook for 15 to 20 minutes, or until golden brown.
10. Take out of the oven. Cool the casserole for 5 minutes before serving.

Nutritional Info	
Fats	27g
Carbs	6.2g
Fiber	2.1g
Protein	33.1g

DOUBLE BACON CHEESEBURGER

Yield: 4 Servings

Requirements:

- 1 pound 80 percent lean ground beef
- 1 shallot, minced
- 1 teaspoon minced garlic
- 1 tablespoon Worcestershire sauce
- ½ teaspoon salt
- ¼ teaspoon freshly ground black pepper
- 4 (1-ounce) slices thick-cut bacon, cooked, grease reserved and cooled
- 1 tablespoon butter
- 4 (1-ounce) slices American cheese
- 4 low-carb buns or lettuce wraps (optional)

Directions:

1. In a large bowl, combine the ground beef, shallot, garlic, Worcestershire sauce, salt, pepper, and reserved bacon grease. Divide the mixture into 4 equal portions and form into patties.
2. In a large cast iron (or other heavy-bottomed) skillet over medium-high heat, heat the butter for 1 minute.
3. Put the patties into the skillet and cook for 3 to 4 minutes. Turn and cook 2 to 3 minutes more for medium-rare.
4. Reduce the heat to medium-low. Place 1 slice of cheese on each patty. Cover the skillet and melt the cheese for 1 to 2 minutes.
5. Take the patties out of the skillet. Top each with 1 slice of bacon.
6. Serve with your favorite condiments, on a low-carb bun, or with a lettuce wrap (if using).

Nutritional Info (1 BACON-AND-CHEESE-TOPPED PATTY)	
Fats	43g
Carbs	3.3g
Fiber	0g
Protein	42.5g

SHRIMP, BAMBOO SHOOT, AND BROCCOLI STIR-FRY

Yield: 2 Servings

Requirements:

- 2 tablespoons olive oil
- ¾ pound shrimp, peeled and deveined
- 1 tablespoon minced garlic
- 1 cup sliced bamboo shoots
- ¼ cup chopped onion
- 1 cup broccoli florets
- ½ teaspoon sesame oil
- 3 tablespoons soy sauce
- ½ teaspoon unsweetened rice wine vinegar
- ½ teaspoon Chinese five-spice powder
- ¼ teaspoon freshly ground black pepper

Directions:

1. Heat a large skillet over medium-high heat. Add the olive oil and heat for 1 minute.
2. Put the shrimp and garlic into the skillet and cook for 2 to 3 minutes, or until the shrimp are almost cooked. Take the shrimp out of the skillet.
3. Reduce the heat to medium. Add the bamboo shoots, onion, and broccoli and sauté for 5 to 8 minutes, or until room temperature. Put in the sesame oil, soy sauce, rice wine vinegar, Chinese five-spice powder, and black pepper. Mix to combine.
4. Place the shrimp back in the skillet, and cook for another 1 to 2 minutes.
5. Serve instantly.

Nutritional Info	
Fats	18.4g
Carbs	10.7g
Fiber	3.5g
Protein	44g

ALMOND BUTTER BREAD

Yield: 12 Servings

Requirements:

- ½ cup unflavored, unsweetened whey protein powder
- ⅛ teaspoon salt
- 2 teaspoons baking powder
- ½ cup unsweetened almond butter
- 4 eggs
- 1 tablespoon butter for loaf pan

Directions:

1. Heat the oven to 300°F.
2. In a small bowl, Combine the whey, salt, and baking powder.
3. In a large bowl, use an electric mixer to whip the almond butter until creamy. Put in one egg at a time, beating well after each addition. Beat the batter until fluffy.
4. Fold the whey mixture into the almond batter. Mix lightly until smooth.
5. Coat the inside of a loaf pan with the tablespoon of butter by rubbing it along the walls and into each corner.
6. Pour the mixture into the loaf pan. Put it in the preheated oven. Bake for 30 to 40 minutes, or until the center is set.
7. Take out of the oven. Cool the loaf for 5 to 10 minutes. Run a knife along the inside edges of the pan to loosen the loaf, and tip the pan upside down to remove it. Put the loaf on a cooling rack to cool completely, about 5 minutes more.
8. Chop the bread, as needed, and refrigerate covered in plastic wrap.

Nutritional Info (1 SLICE)	
Fats	7.6g
Carbs	2.4g
Fiber	0.4g
Protein	6.5g

BACON-WRAPPED SCALLOPS AND BROCCOLINI

Yield: 3 Servings

Requirements:

- 5 bacon slices
- 1 pound scallops (about 10)
- ½ teaspoon salt, divided
- ¼ teaspoon freshly ground black pepper, divided
- 4 tablespoons (½ stick) butter, divided
- 15 broccolini pieces
- 1 teaspoon minced garlic
- 2 tablespoons dry white wine
- 2 teaspoons olive oil

Directions:

1. Chop the bacon slices in half crosswise, creating 10 small slices. Wrap one slice around each scallop, locked with a toothpick. Sprinkle with ¼ teaspoon of salt and ⅛ teaspoon of pepper.
2. Heat a medium skillet over medium-high heat. Put in 3 tablespoons of butter and heat for 2 minutes.
3. Put in the broccolini, garlic, and wine. Sauté for 2 minutes. Cover and lower the heat to medium-low.
4. Heat a large skillet over medium-high heat. Put in the remaining tablespoon of butter and the olive oil and heat for 2 minutes.
5. Raise the heat under the large skillet to high. Put in the scallops. Sear for 1½ minutes per side. Turn the scallops onto their sides so the bacon crisps and cook for about 1 minute on each side.
6. Check the broccolini for doneness. Sprinkle with the remaining ¼ teaspoon of salt and ⅛ teaspoon of pepper.

7. Plate instantly with the scallops, saucing with any excess garlic butter from the pan.

Nutritional Info (3 BACON-WRAPPED SCALLOPS)	
Fats	35.5g
Carbs	7.9g
Fiber	1g
Protein	41.5g

COCONUT ALMOND FLOUR BREAD

Yield: 12 Servings

Requirements:

- 10 tablespoons butter, melted, plus 1 tablespoon for the loaf pan
- 1 tablespoon honey
- 1½ tablespoons apple cider vinegar
- 8 eggs
- ¾ cup almond flour
- ¾ teaspoon baking soda
- ¾ teaspoon salt
- ⅔ cup coconut flour
- Preheat your oven to 300°F.

Directions:

1. In a small bowl, combine the butter, honey, and cider vinegar. Allow the mixture to cool.
2. In a medium bowl, beat the eggs.
3. Put the almond flour, butter mixture, baking soda, and salt into the eggs. Mix well with a hand mixer.
4. Carefully sift the coconut flour into the bowl. Mix thoroughly to combine.
5. Coat the inside of a loaf pan with 1 tablespoon of butter by rubbing it along the walls and into each corner.
6. Pour the mixture into the loaf pan. Lay it in the preheated oven. Bake for 50 to 60 minutes, until the center is set.
7. Take the pan out of the oven. Let it to cool for at least 15 minutes.
8. Run a knife along the inside edges of the pan to loosen the loaf, and tip the pan upside down to remove it. Put the bread on a cooling rack to cool completely, about 5 minutes more.

9. Chop the bread into 12 slices, and refrigerate covered in plastic wrap.

Nutritional Info (1 SLICE)	
Fats	17.2g
Carbs	3.5g
Fiber	3g
Protein	5g

BACON-WRAPPED JALAPEÑO CHICKEN

Yield: 4 Servings

Requirements:

- 4 (4-ounce) boneless chicken breasts
- ¾ cup cream cheese, at room temperature
- 4 jalapeño peppers, halved
- 1 teaspoon onion powder
- 2 garlic cloves, minced
- 8 bacon slices
- ¼ teaspoon salt
- ⅛ teaspoon freshly ground black pepper
- 2 tablespoons olive oil

Directions:

1.   Preheat your oven to 400°F.
2.   On a flat surface, slice each chicken breast in half horizontally. Do not cut all the way through the other side. Open the breasts flat.
3.   Spread the same amount of cream cheese over each of the butterflied breasts.
4.   Top each with two jalapeño halves. Season with onion powder and garlic.
5.   Fold the breasts closed. Cover each breast with two bacon slices. Lock with toothpicks. Sprinkle the outside of the breasts with the salt and pepper.
6.   Lay the bacon-wrapped chicken in a baking pan. Lightly sprinkle with the olive oil.
7.   Place the pan into the preheated oven. Bake the chicken for 20 minutes, or until the internal temperature is 165°F.
8.   Take the pan out of the oven. Let the chicken rest for 2 to 3 minutes. Take the toothpicks out of the meat and serve.

Nutritional Info	
Fats	42.2g
Carbs	3.3g
Fiber	0.5g
Protein	47g

CRAB CAKES WITH GARLIC AIOLI

Yield: 4 Servings

Requirements:

FOR THE CRAB CAKES

- ½ pound jumbo lump crabmeat
- ½ pound lump crabmeat
- ¼ cup mayonnaise
- 1 egg, beaten
- ¼ cup coconut flour
- 1 teaspoon mustard
- 1 teaspoon seafood seasoning
- ¼ teaspoon paprika
- 1 teaspoon minced garlic
- ¼ cup finely chopped onion
- ¼ cup finely chopped bell pepper
- 1 tablespoon finely chopped fresh parsley
- ¼ teaspoon salt
- ¼ teaspoon freshly ground black pepper
- 1 cup shredded Parmesan cheese
- 3 tablespoons butter

FOR THE AIOLI

- 2 teaspoons minced garlic
- 1 tablespoon freshly squeezed lemon juice
- 1 egg
- ½ teaspoon salt
- ⅛ teaspoon freshly ground black pepper
- ½ cup olive oil

Directions:

To make the crab cakes

1.   In a large bowl, mix together the jumbo lump crabmeat, lump crabmeat, mayonnaise, egg, coconut flour, mustard, seafood seasoning, paprika, garlic, onion, bell pepper, parsley, salt, and pepper. Mix thoroughly.
2.   Add in the Parmesan cheese and mix. Split the crabmeat mixture into six equal portions. Make each into a patty. Refrigerate to firm up while making the aioli.

To make the aioli

1.   In a food processor, combine the garlic and lemon juice and process until smooth and.
2.   Put in the egg, salt, and pepper. Purée, while slowly adding the olive oil until the aioli forms. Set aside.

To finish the dish

1.   Heat a large skillet over medium-high heat. Put in the butter and cook for 1 minute.
2.   Slowly add the crab cakes to the pan and cook for 7 minutes, being cautious not to burn the butter. Lower the heat to medium. Turn the cakes and cook for 5 to 7 minutes more, or until done. Transfer the crab cakes to paper towels to drain.
3.   Serve instantly with half of the aioli. Refrigerate the remaining aioli stored in an airtight container.

Nutritional Info	
Fats	46g
Carbs	7.5g

Fiber	3g
Protein	32g

CHEESY TACO SHELLS

Yield: 1 Servings

Requirements:

- ½ cup shredded Mexican cheese blend, divided
- ¼ teaspoon garlic salt

Directions:

1. On a waxed paper plate, arrange ¼ cup of cheese so it coats the entire plate to the edges. Sprinkle the garlic salt on top.
2. Lay the plate in the microwave. Heat on high for 1½ minutes, or until the cheese has melted and is brown around the edges and golden in the middle.
3. Take the plate out of the microwave. With a knife, gently remove the melted cheese disk from the plate. Wrap it over the edge of a cutting board placed on its side. The cheese should be wrapped evenly.
4. Let it to set for 3 to 5 minutes before moving. Do it again with the remaining ¼ cup of cheese.
5. Fill the taco shells with any preferred ingredients and enjoy.

Nutritional Info (2 SHELLS)	
Fats	20g
Carbs	3.1g
Fiber	0g
Protein	14g

136

PARMESAN-CRUSTED TILAPIA WITH SAUTÉED SPINACH

Yield: 2 Servings

Requirements:

- ½ cup grated Parmesan cheese
- 2 tablespoons almond flour
- 1 teaspoon paprika
- ¼ teaspoon salt
- ⅛ teaspoon freshly ground black pepper
- 2 tilapia fillets
- 2 tablespoons olive oil, divided
- 1½ cups spinach
- ½ teaspoon garlic powder
- 1 tablespoon chopped fresh parsley

Directions:

1. Preheat your oven to 400°F.
2. In a medium bowl, combine the Parmesan cheese, almond flour, paprika, salt, and pepper.
3. Put the tilapia fillets on a plate and drizzle with 1 tablespoon of olive oil.
4. Massage the oil into the fish, and then dip them in the Parmesan mix, coating completely.
5. Coat a baking dish with aluminum foil. Lay the fillets inside. Place the dish in the preheated oven and bake for 10 to 15 minutes, depending on the thickness of the fillets.
6. While the fillets cook, Put in the remaining tablespoon of olive oil to a large skillet and heat over medium-high heat.
7. Put in the spinach and sauté until tender, about 6 minutes.

8. Put in the garlic powder. Cover, and lower the heat to medium-low and cook for 3 to 5 minutes.

9. Tale the baking dish out of the oven. Check the fillets for doneness.

10. Plate the spinach with the fillets on top and serve instantly, garnished with the parsley.

Nutritional Info PER SERVING (1 TILAPIA FILLET, ½ OF THE SPINACH)	
Fats	27g
Carbs	4g
Fiber	1.7g
Protein	32g

Week 4 Diet Plan

	Breakfast	Lunch	Dinner
M O N	**CREAM CHEESE PANCAKES** (Pg 140)	**FETA AND OLIVE STUFFED CHICKEN THIGHS (Pg 150)**	**GRILLED SHRIMP WITH AVOCADO SALAD** (Pg 163)
T U E	**Chorizo Breakfast Casserole (Pg 141)**	**STEAMED MUSSELS WITH GARLIC AND THYME** (Pg 155)	**CHICKEN PICCATA** (Pg 165)
W E D	**RASPBERRY SCONES** (Pg 143)	**CAULIFLOWER MAC AND CHEESE** (Pg 153)	**BARBECUE PORK RIBS** (Pg 167)
T H U	**Lettuce Breakfast Taco** (Pg 144)	**STUFFED BONE-IN PORK CHOPS** (Pg 155)	**CAULIFLOWER TORTILLAS** (Pg 169)
F R I	**WAFFLES WITH WHIPPED CREAM (Pg 145)**	**CHICKEN THIGHS WITH LEMON CREAM SAUCE** (Pg 157)	**CHEESY-CRUST PIZZA** (Pg 171)
S A T	**Breakfast Quiche (Pg 147)**	**COCONUT SHRIMP** (Pg 159)	**SHRIMP SCAMPI WITH ZUCCHINI NOODLES** (Pg 173)
S U N	**CINNAMON MUFFINS WITH CREAM CHEESE (Pg 148)**	**CAULIFLOWER MASH** (Pg 161)	**BAKED CHICKEN TENDERS** (Pg 175)

Week 4 Cookbook

CREAM CHEESE PANCAKES

Yield: 1 Serving

Requirements:

- ¼ cup cream cheese, at room temperature
- 2 eggs
- ½ teaspoon stevia
- ¼ teaspoon nutmeg

Directions:

1. Heat a griddle over medium-low heat.
2. Put the cream cheese in a blender. Add the eggs, stevia, and nutmeg and pulse until the batter is smooth.
3. Gradually pour a small amount of the batter onto the griddle, about one-eighth cup per pancake. The batter will be very thin and spread effortlessly.
4. Cook the pancake for just over 1 minute before gently turning and cook for another minute before removing from the pan.
5. Replicate the process with the remaining batter.

Nutritional Info PER SERVING (6 TO 8 PANCAKES)	
Fats	29g
Carbs	2.5g
Fiber	0g
Protein	15.4g

Chorizo Breakfast Casserole

Yield: 10 Servings

Requirements:

- 16 Oz Ground Chorizo
- 110 g Onion (1 small)
- 145 g Green Pepper (1 small)
- 366 g Spinach
- 180 g Heavy Cream (12 Tbsp)
- 12 eggs
- 1 tsp Garlic Powder, Onion Powder, Salt, Pepper
- 8 Oz Cheddar
- 9 Oz Cherry Tomatoes

Directions:

1. Cook the spinach in the microwave.
2. Grind up or slice the chorizo and cook in a skillet until browned.
3. Place finished chorizo in a large bowl.
4. Finely slice 1 onion and 1 pepper, cook in the same skillet, when done put in the large bowl.
5. When the spinach is done, Place into the bowl.
6. Mix together the 12 eggs, heavy cream and spices.
7. Add the cheese to the bowl and combine, then add the egg mixture and combine.
8. Transfer to a greased casserole dish.
9. Add cherry tomatoes if you wish.
10. Cook at 350 degrees for 50 minutes.

Nutritional Info	
Fats	28g
Carbs	7g
Fiber	2g
Protein	24g

RASPBERRY SCONES

Yield: 8 Servings

Requirements:

- 1 cup almond flour
- 2 eggs, beaten
- ⅓ cup Splenda, stevia, or other sugar substitute
- 1½ teaspoons pure vanilla extract
- 1½ teaspoons baking powder
- ½ cup raspberries

Directions:

1. Preheat your oven to 375°F.
2. Coat a baking sheet with parchment paper.
3. In a large bowl, mix together the almond flour, eggs, Splenda, vanilla, and baking powder. Mix thoroughly.
4. Put in the raspberries to the bowl and gently fold in.
5. After the raspberries are added, spoon 2 to 3 tablespoons of the batter, per scone, onto the parchment-lined baking sheet.
6. Lay the baking sheet into the preheated oven. Bake for 15 minutes, or until lightly browned.
7. Take the baking sheet out of the oven. Place the scones on a rack to cool for 10 minutes.

Nutritional Info (1 SCONE)	
Fats	8.6g
Carbs	4g
Fiber	2g
Protein	1.5g

Lettuce Breakfast Taco

Yield: 2 Servings

Requirements:

- 2 Romaine Lettuce Leafs
- 4 Large Eggs
- 2 Tbsp Heavy Cream
- 4-6 slices Bacon
- 2 Tbsp Shredded Cheddar
- 2 slices Cheddar Cheese
- To Taste Salt, Pepper, Onion Powder

Directions:

1. Cook the bacon to preferred doness.
2. Mix Eggs, Cream and seasonings.
3. Scramble eggs, mix in cheese at the end.
4. Mix Eggs, Bacon and Cheese into Lettuce.
5. Serve.

Nutritional Info	
Fats	40g
Carbs	3g
Fiber	1g
Protein	29g

WAFFLES WITH WHIPPED CREAM

Yield: 4 TO 5 WAFFLES

Requirements:

FOR THE WAFFLES

- Cooking spray for waffle iron
- ¼ cup coconut flour
- ¼ cup almond flour
- ¼ cup flax meal
- 1 teaspoon baking powder
- 1 teaspoon stevia, or other sugar substitute
- ¼ teaspoon cinnamon
- ¾ cup egg whites (about 3 whites)
- 4 whole eggs
- 1 teaspoon pure vanilla extract

FOR THE WHIPPED CREAM

- ½ cup heavy (whipping) cream
- 1 teaspoon stevia, or other sugar substitute

Directions:

To make the waffles

1. Heat the waffle iron to medium-high heat.
2. Coat with cooking spray.
3. In a large bowl, whisk together the coconut flour, almond flour, flax meal, baking powder, stevia, and cinnamon.
4. In another medium bowl, beat the egg whites until stiff peaks form.
5. Put the whole eggs and vanilla into the dry ingredients and mix thoroughly.

6. Carefully fold the beaten egg whites into the dry ingredients until fully incorporated.
7. Pour the batter onto the preheated waffle iron and cook according to waffle iron directions.

To make the whipped cream

1. In a medium bowl, whip the heavy cream for 3 to 4 minutes, until thick.
2. Put in the stevia. Continue to whisk until stiff peaks form, about 1 minute more.
3. Top the waffles with equal amounts of the whipped cream and serve.

Nutritional Info PER SERVING (2 WAFFLES, ½ OF THE WHIPPED CREAM)	
Fats	27g
Carbs	6.5g
Fiber	9.2g
Protein	27g

Breakfast Quiche

Yield: 10 Servings

Requirements:

- 12 Eggs (8 eggs for smaller pan)
- 10 Bacon
- 450g Broccoli (whole bag)
- 2g Spinach
- 1 Cup Heavy Cream (1/2c for smaller pan)
- 10 oz Grape Tomatoes
- 5 oz Cheddar Cheese (hand grate)
- To taste Salt, pepper and garlic powder

Directions:

1. Fry bacon and set aside.
2. Fry vegetables in bacon grease (don't fry tomatoes).
3. Spread fried vegetables in pan.
4. Whisk eggs, spices and cream together and pour over vegetables.
5. Crumble bacon over mixture, distribute cheese and tomatoes; pack mixture down.
6. Bake at 375 for 40 minutes (30 for smaller pan).
7. Chop it up and eat it for breakfast for as long as it lasts.

Nutritional Info	
Fats	24g
Carbs	8g
Fiber	5g
Protein	17g

CINNAMON MUFFINS WITH CREAM CHEESE FROSTING

Yield: 12 Servings

Requirements:

FOR THE CINNAMON MUFFINS

- 1 cup almond flour
- ½ cup coconut flour
- 2 teaspoons baking powder
- ¼ cup erythritol, or other sugar substitute, like stevia
- 6 eggs
- ½ cup butter, melted
- ½ cup sparkling water
- 1 teaspoon pure vanilla extract
- 1½ tablespoons cinnamon

FOR THE CREAM CHEESE FROSTING

- 8 ounces (1 package) cream cheese, at room temperature
- 1 tablespoon sour cream
- ½ teaspoon pure vanilla extract

Directions:

To make the cinnamon muffins

1. Preheat your oven to 350°F.
2. In a medium bowl, Combine the almond flour, coconut flour, baking powder, and Erythritol and mix.
3. In a large bowl, whisk the eggs. Put in the melted butter, sparkling water, and vanilla. Mix to combine.
4. Put the dry ingredients into the wet ingredients. Mix thoroughly.

5. Spoon the batter uniformly into a cupcake pan. Top each muffin with an equal amount of cinnamon.

6. Using a toothpick, swirl the cinnamon into the batter.

7. Lay the cupcake pan in the preheated oven. Bake for 20 to 25 minutes, or until golden brown.

8. Take the cupcake out of the oven and cool the muffins in the pan for 5 to 10 minutes.

To make the cream cheese frosting

1. In a medium bowl, thoroughly mix the cream cheese, sour cream, and vanilla.

2. Refrigerate until needed. Distribute uniformly on the muffins before serving.

Nutritional Info (1 MUFFIN WITH CREAM CHEESE FROSTING)	
Fats	18.5g
Carbs	3.1g
Fiber	3g
Protein	5.3g

FETA AND OLIVE STUFFED CHICKEN THIGHS

Yield: 4 Servings

Requirements:

- 1 cup crumbled feta cheese
- ¼ cup shredded Swiss cheese
- 1 teaspoon minced garlic
- 1 tablespoon olive oil
- ¼ cup olives, chopped
- 1 pound boneless chicken thighs
- ¼ teaspoon salt
- ¼ teaspoon freshly ground black pepper

Directions:

1.   Preheat your oven to 425°F. In a large bowl, combine the feta cheese, Swiss cheese, garlic, olive oil, and olives.

2.   On a flat surface, lay out the chicken thighs. Spread the meat open so the thighs lay flat. Put the same amount of the feta mixture on each piece of chicken. Close the thighs. Lock with toothpicks. Sprinkle with the salt and pepper.

3.   Lay the chicken in a baking dish. Place the dish into the preheated oven and bake for about 18 minutes. Serve when the meat thermometer shows an internal temperature of 165°F.

Nutritional Info	
Fats	31g
Carbs	2.3g
Fiber	0.4g
Protein	27.3g

STEAMED MUSSELS WITH GARLIC AND THYME

Yield: Servings 8

Requirements:

- 4 pounds live mussels, cleaned, scrubbed, and debearded
- ½ cup butter
- 3 tablespoons olive oil
- ½ cup diced onion
- 4 garlic cloves, minced
- ½ cup diced tomato
- 1 tablespoon fresh thyme
- ½ cup white wine
- 1 cup chicken or seafood broth
- 2 tablespoons freshly squeezed lemon juice
- ½ teaspoon salt
- ¼ teaspoon freshly ground black pepper

Directions:

1. Put the cleaned mussels in a large bowl. Cover with cool water. Set aside.
2. In a large, heavy pot over medium heat, heat the butter and olive oil for about 1 minute. Put in the onions and cook for 3 to 5 minutes, until translucent. Put in the garlic and cook for 1 to 2 minutes more.
3. Put in the tomato, thyme, white wine, broth, lemon juice, salt, and pepper.
4. Raise the heat and bring the mixture to a boil.
5. Put in the mussels and cover the pot and cook for 8 to 10 minutes, shaking the pot occasionally to let the mussels to cook evenly.
6. Pour the steaming mussels into a bowl. Discard any that are unopened.
7. Serve instantly.

Nutritional Info	
Fats	22.5g
Carbs	11g
Fiber	0.5g
Protein	28.4g

CAULIFLOWER MAC AND CHEESE

Yield: Servings 8

Requirements:

- 1 teaspoon salt, divided
- 1 head fresh cauliflower, chopped into small florets
- 1 cup heavy (whipping) cream
- ⅓ cup cream cheese, cubed
- 1 cup shredded Cheddar cheese
- ½ cup shredded mozzarella cheese
- ½ teaspoon minced garlic
- ¼ teaspoon freshly ground black pepper
- Cooking spray for baking pan
- ½ cup shredded Parmesan cheese

Directions:

1. Preheat your oven to 400°F.
2. Bring a large pot of water to a boil. Sprinkle with ½ teaspoon of salt.
3. Cautiously drop the cauliflower into the boiling water and cook for 5 minutes.
4. Drain completely, and place the florets on paper towels to absorb any remaining moisture. Place the cauliflower in a large bowl and set aside.
5. Add the heavy cream to a large skillet over medium heat, and bring to a simmer. Mix in the cream cheese and whisk or stir until smooth. Put in the Cheddar cheese, mozzarella cheese, and garlic. Whisk until the cheeses melt, about 2 minutes.
6. Take the cheese sauce out of the heat and pour over the cauliflower. Stir to cover the florets evenly. Season with the remaining ½ teaspoon of salt and the pepper.
7. Sprinkle an 8-inch-square baking pan with cooking spray. Transfer the cauliflower mixture to the pan. Top with the Parmesan cheese.

8. Lay the pan in the preheated oven. Bake for 20 minutes, or until the top is browned.
9. Cool for 5 minutes before serving.

Nutritional Info	
Fats	17g
Carbs	2.4g
Fiber	1g
Protein	10g

STUFFED BONE-IN PORK CHOPS

Yield: Servings 2

Requirements:

FOR THE STUFFING

- 2 tablespoons olive oil, divided
- 1 teaspoon minced garlic
- 3 tablespoons finely chopped onion
- ⅓ cup spinach
- 2 ounces Muenster cheese, shredded
- 1 egg, beaten

FOR THE PORK CHOPS

- 2 (6- to 8-ounce) bone-in pork chops
- ½ teaspoon salt
- ¼ teaspoon finely ground black pepper

Directions:

To make the stuffing

1. In a large oven-safe skillet over medium-high heat, heat 1 tablespoon of olive oil for 1 minute. Add the garlic and sauté until fragrant, about 1 minute.
2. Add the onion and spinach. Lower the heat to medium and cook for 2 to 3 minutes. Transfer the mixture to a small bowl to cool.
3. Once cooled, add the Muenster cheese and the egg. Mix well to combine.

To make the pork chops

1. Preheat your oven to 375°F.
2. On a flat surface, Slice the pork chops through the middle horizontally to the bone. Open the meat up. Stuff half of the spinach mixture into each pork

chop. Fold the chop together over the stuffing and lock the edges with toothpicks, if needed. Sprinkle with the salt and pepper.

3. In the large oven-safe skillet, heat the left over tablespoon of olive oil over medium-high heat. Put the chops into the skillet and cook each side for 2 minutes. Once cooked, Take the skillet off the heat and place it into the preheated oven. Bake for 15 minutes, or until the internal temperature reaches 150°F.

4. Serve with your preferred side dishes.

Nutritional Info (1 STUFFED PORK CHOP)	
Fats	44.5g
Carbs	4g
Fiber	1.4g
Protein	45.5g

CHICKEN THIGHS WITH LEMON CREAM SAUCE

Yield: Servings 4

Requirements:

- 1 tablespoon butter
- 1 tablespoon minced shallots
- 1 cup sour cream
- 2 tablespoons freshly squeezed lemon juice
- ½ teaspoon salt, divided
- ¼ teaspoon freshly ground black pepper, divided
- 1 pound bone-in chicken thighs

Directions:

1. Preheat your oven to 425°F.

2. In a large skillet over medium-low heat, melt the butter. Put in the shallots.

3. Cook for 3 to 4 minutes, or until tender. Reduce the heat to low. Put in the sour cream, lemon juice, ¼ teaspoon of salt, and ⅛ teaspoon of pepper. Mix thoroughly. Refrigerate until ready to serve.

4. Sprinkle the chicken with the remaining ¼ teaspoon of salt and ⅛ teaspoon of pepper.

5. Lay the chicken into a baking dish and into the preheated oven. Bake for about 18 minutes. With a meat thermometer, check the internal temperature. It should reach 165°F.

6. Plate the chicken, spooning an equal amount of lemon cream sauce on each thigh.

Nutritional Info

Fats	32g
Carbs	3g
Fiber	0g
Protein	22g

COCONUT SHRIMP

Yield: Servings 6

Requirements:

FOR THE COCONUT SHRIMP

- Oil for frying
- 1 cup unsweetened shredded coconut
- ½ cup unsweetened flaked coconut
- ¼ cup unsweetened coconut milk
- ½ cup mayonnaise
- 2 egg yolks
- ¼ teaspoon salt
- ⅛ teaspoon freshly ground black pepper
- ½ teaspoon garlic powder
- 1 pound shrimp, peeled and deveined, tails left on

FOR THE AIOLI

- ½ cup mayonnaise
- 2 tablespoons chili sauce, such as Huy Fong Foods brand
- 2 teaspoons freshly squeezed lime juice
- 1 teaspoon red pepper flakes

Directions:

To make the coconut shrimp

1. In a large pot, heat 2 inches of oil to 350°F for deep-frying.
2. In a medium bowl, combine the shredded coconut, flaked coconut, coconut milk, mayonnaise, egg yolks, salt, pepper, and garlic powder and mix well.

3. Using 1 to 2 tablespoons of batter, cautiously form it around each shrimp, leaving the tails exposed.
4. Instantly drop the battered shrimp into the preheated oil. Repeat with 2 to 3 more shrimp and cook for 4 to 6 minutes, until golden brown.
5. Take the shrimp out of the oil. Set aside to cool on a paper-towel-lined plate. Repeat the process with the remaining shrimp.

To make the aioli

1. In a small bowl, thoroughly mix the mayonnaise, chili sauce, lime juice, and red pepper flakes.
2. Serve instantly with the coconut shrimp.

Nutritional Info	
Fats	41g
Carbs	3.8g
Fiber	2.2g
Protein	19g

CAULIFLOWER MASH

Yield: Servings 6

Requirements:

- 3 cups cauliflower florets
- 6 tablespoons butter
- 4 tablespoons grated Parmesan cheese
- 2 tablespoons sour cream
- 2 tablespoons cream cheese
- 2 tablespoons heavy (whipping) cream
- 1 teaspoon minced garlic
- 1 teaspoon salt
- ½ teaspoon freshly ground black pepper

Directions:

1. Bring a large pot of water to a rolling boil. Put in the cauliflower florets.
2. Cook for 4 to 5 minutes. Drain the cooked cauliflower, pressing out any surplus moisture.
3. In the bowl of a food processor, mix the cauliflower florets, butter, Parmesan cheese, sour cream, cream cheese, heavy cream, garlic, salt, and pepper.
4. Pulse to combine and mix until smooth.

Nutritional Info	
Fats	19.5g
Carbs	4g
Fiber	1.g
Protein	7.7g

GRILLED SHRIMP WITH AVOCADO SALAD

Yield: Servings 3

Requirements:

- 1 pound shrimp, peeled and deveined
- 2 tablespoons olive oil
- ½ teaspoon garlic powder
- ½ teaspoon salt, divided
- ⅛ teaspoon freshly ground black pepper
- 1 avocado, peeled, pitted, and diced
- ¼ cup chopped bell pepper
- ¼ cup chopped tomato
- ¼ cup chopped onion
- 1 teaspoon freshly squeezed lime juice

Directions:

1. Heat a griddle over medium-high heat.
2. In a large bowl, mix the shrimp, olive oil, garlic powder, ¼ teaspoon of salt, and pepper. Mix until the shrimp are coated completely.
3. In a medium bowl, mix together the avocado, bell pepper, tomato, onion, and lime juice. Season with the remaining ¼ teaspoon of salt. Set aside in the refrigerator.
4. Lay the shrimp on the hot griddle, on their sides and cook for 2 to 3 minutes.
5. Turn, and cook for another 1 to 2 minutes. Take the shrimp out of the griddle.
6. Plate with the avocado salad to serve.

Nutritional Info	
Fats	25g
Carbs	10.9g
Fiber	5.8g
Protein	36.1g

CHICKEN PICCATA

Yield: 4 Servings

Requirements:

- 1 pound boneless chicken thighs
- ¼ teaspoon salt
- ⅛ teaspoon freshly ground black pepper
- ¼ cup olive oil
- ½ cup dry white wine
- 1 tablespoon freshly squeezed lemon juice
- 1 garlic clove, minced
- 1 tablespoon capers, chopped
- 3 tablespoons chopped fresh parsley

Directions:

1. On a flat surface, flatten the chicken thighs with a meat tenderizer until they are ¼ inch thick. Sprinkle with the salt and pepper.
2. In a large skillet over medium heat, heat the olive oil for about 1 minute.
3. Lay two chicken thighs in the pan and cook for about 4 minutes per side. Place in a plate. Do again, two at a time, with the remaining thighs. Set aside.
4. Using the same skillet, raise the heat to high. Put in the white wine, lemon juice, garlic, and capers. Stir the sauce, scraping any browned bits from the bottom of the pan. Bring to a boil and cook for 1 minute.
5. Put the chicken back into the pan. Heat in the sauce for 1 minute.
6. Put in the parsley and stir to incorporate before serving.

Nutritional Info	
Fats	30g
Carbs	1.4g
Fiber	0g
Protein	20g

BARBECUE PORK RIBS

Yield: Servings 5

Requirements:

FOR THE RUB

- ¼ cup olive oil
- 2 garlic cloves, minced
- 1 shallot, minced
- 1 teaspoon cumin
- 1 teaspoon paprika
- 1 teaspoon chili powder
- 1 teaspoon salt
- ½ teaspoon cayenne pepper
- ½ teaspoon freshly ground black pepper
- ¼ teaspoon ground ginger

FOR THE RIBS

- 2 pounds baby back pork rib racks
- Barbecue Sauce , or purchased sugar-free barbecue sauce (optional)

Directions:

To make the rub

1. In a blender or food processor, combine the olive oil, garlic, shallot, cumin, paprika, chili powder, salt, cayenne pepper, black pepper, and ginger.
2. Process until mixed thoroughly.

To make the ribs

1. On a flat surface, chop the rib racks into quarters and arrange on a baking sheet. Cover the ribs uniformly with the rub, massaging it into the meat. Refrigerate the ribs to marinate for at least 4 hours.
2. Preheat your oven to 300°F.
3. Put the ribs in the oven and cook for 1 hour, 10 minutes.
4. Take the ribs out of the oven. Let them cool for 2 to 3 minutes before slicing.
5. Serve!

Nutritional Info	
Fats	54g
Carbs	1.8g
Fiber	0.5g
Protein	30g

CAULIFLOWER TORTILLAS

Yield: 6 Servings

Requirements:

- ¾ head fresh cauliflower
- 2 eggs
- ½ teaspoon salt
- ¼ teaspoon freshly ground black pepper

Directions:

1. Preheat your oven to 375°F.
2. Put the cauliflower in a food processor and pulse into very fine pieces.
3. In a large microwaveable bowl, microwave the prepared cauliflower on high, about 5 minutes. Stir the cauliflower and microwave for 2 minutes more.
4. Stir it again.
5. Using a dish towel or cheesecloth, drain all the surplus water from the cauliflower.
6. Place the cauliflower back into the bowl. Put in the eggs, salt, and pepper. Mix thoroughly.
7. On a parchment-lined baking sheet, use your hands to spread the mixture into 6 or 7 small circles, flattening them gently.
8. Place the sheet into the preheated oven. Bake for 10 minutes.
9. Take the sheet out of the oven. Cautiously remove the cauliflower tortillas from the parchment and flip them. Place the tortillas back into the oven and bake for 6 to 7 minutes more.
10. Crisp, as needed, in a lightly oiled skillet before serving.

Nutritional Info (1 TORTILLA)	
Fats	1.5g
Carbs	2g
Fiber	1.7g
Protein	3.2g

CHEESY-CRUST PIZZA

Yield: Servings 4

Requirements:

- 1½ cups shredded mozzarella cheese, divided
- ½ cup Cheddar cheese
- 1 egg
- ½ teaspoon garlic powder
- ¼ teaspoon salt
- ⅛ teaspoon freshly ground black pepper
- ¼ cup sugar-free pizza sauce
- 20 pepperoni slices

Directions:

1. Preheat your oven to 450°F.
2. In a large bowl, mix 1 cup of mozzarella cheese, the Cheddar cheese, egg, garlic powder, salt, and pepper.
3. On a parchment-lined 16-inch pizza pan, spread the cheese dough uniformly around the pan. The crust should be slim, but without any holes.
4. Lay the pan in the oven. Bake the crust for 15 to 20 minutes, or until browned. Check the oven after 10 minutes to make sure it's not burning.
5. Take the crust out of the oven. Turn the oven to broil.
6. With paper towels, remove any surplus grease from the crust.
7. Spread the sauce over the crust. Top with the remaining ½ cup of mozzarella cheese and the pepperoni.
8. Place the pan back into the oven. Bake for 3 to 4 minutes, or until the cheese is melted and bubbling.
9. Take the pan out of the oven. Cool the pizza for 3 to 5 minutes before slicing and serving.

Nutritional Info (¼ Of 16-INCH PIZZA)	
Fats	26.6g
Carbs	3.8g
Fiber	0g
Protein	24g

SHRIMP SCAMPI WITH ZUCCHINI NOODLES

Yield: 3 Servings

Requirements:

- 2 tablespoons olive oil
- 1 tablespoon minced garlic
- 1 pound shrimp, peeled and deveined
- ¼ cup dry white wine
- 2 tablespoons freshly squeezed lemon juice
- 1 tablespoon butter
- 3 tablespoons heavy (whipping) cream
- 2½ cups zucchini noodles
- ¼ teaspoon salt
- ¼ teaspoon freshly ground black pepper
- 1 tablespoon chopped fresh parsley

Directions:

1. Heat a large skillet over medium heat. Add the olive oil and heat for about 1 minute. Add the garlic and cook for 1 minute.
2. Add the shrimp to the pan and cook on all sides, turning, about 4 minutes.
3. Remove the shrimp from the pan. Set aside, leaving the liquid in the pan.
4. To the pan with the reserved liquid, add the white wine and lemon juice.
5. Scrape the bottom of the pan to incorporate any solids with the liquid, stirring constantly for 2 minutes.
6. Add the butter and heavy cream and cook for 1 minute.
7. Add the zucchini noodles to the pan and cook, stirring occasionally, for about 2 minutes or until the zucchini is al dente (noodle-like) in texture.
8. Return the shrimp to the pan. Season with the salt and pepper. Stir to incorporate all ingredients.

9. Plate and garnish with fresh parsley. Serve instantly.

Nutritional Info	
Fats	22g
Carbs	6.5g
Fiber	1.2g
Protein	36g

BAKED CHICKEN TENDERS

Yield: 4 Servings

Requirements:

- 2 eggs
- ½ cup pork rinds, ground
- ½ cup shredded Parmesan cheese
- 1 teaspoon garlic powder
- 1 teaspoon onion powder
- ¼ teaspoon salt
- ⅛ teaspoon freshly ground black pepper
- 1 pound boneless chicken thighs, halved

Directions:

1. Preheat your oven to 400°F.
2. Cover a baking sheet with parchment paper.
3. In a medium bowl, beat the eggs.
4. In another medium bowl, mix the pork rinds, Parmesan cheese, garlic powder, onion powder, salt, and pepper.
5. Line up the egg wash, then the pork rind mixture, then the baking sheet.
6. Take one thigh half and dip thoroughly in the egg wash, then coat in the pork rind mixture, pressing the coating into the meat so it sticks. Place the coated thigh on the baking sheet. Do again with the remaining thigh halves.
7. Put the baking sheet in the preheated oven and cook for 18 to 20 minutes, or until golden brown.

Nutritional Info	
Fats	33g
Carbs	2.2g
Fiber	0g
Protein	49g

ENDNOTE

Thank you for purchasing this book. I hope it helps you achieve your fitness goals and lose that unwanted fat. Good Luck!! Have Fun!!

21673028R00104

Made in the USA
Middletown, DE
07 July 2015